STUDY AND LIKE IT

STUDY
and Like It

John J. Vogel, Ph.D.

An Exposition-University Book

Exposition Press   **Hicksville, New York**

This book is gratefully dedicated

to the memory of

my father and mother,

my first and best teachers

Contents

Preface

Like any other instructor I have often been frustrated at the careless, inefficient way in which many students "bang away" at their studying. I have at times, as my students will remember, chided them "for not knowing how to study," but with what effect they alone can say. One day the thought came to me: Perhaps they do not know how to study because no one has taught them how. By way of an experiment, I then offered to give a series of informal instructions on how to study. Only a few of them accepted the offer, but as the instructions continued, the material under treatment grew to an extent quite beyond my original anticipation. Then I enlarged and completely overhauled the entire material. When this was done I found myself with a stack of manuscripts which I merely laid away in my files and forgot that I had even written. Recently I casually opened my file cabinet, read the forgotten manuscripts and then decided to publish them under the title *Study and Like It.*

If throughout these pages I address myself directly to college students, it is only because this class of students was uppermost in my mind while I wrote. But the principles set forth in this volume are equally suited to high school students, or to postgraduate students or to students everywhere—in fact, to all who regard studying and learning seriously regardless of their status or age.

Practically all the problems and difficulties encountered by an earnest student are treated in this book. But I have designedly stripped these pages of statistical tables, detailed data of educational experiments and all unnecessary technical expressions, which are often more wearisome than enlightening for the ordinary reader. As the title clearly suggests, I believe that studying and learning at any time of life can be an enjoyable and stimulating venture. But nowhere do I cozen the idea that studying is a "snap" or that there is any enchanted shortcut to learning. On the contrary, I assure without apology that study is labor requiring determination and pluck, but that it can be pleasant and interesting nevertheless. So I have endeavored to make these pages inspirational as well as informational. The reader will recognize that many suggestions and recommendations appearing in this book are my personal opinions. These are merely offered for what they are worth.

The sequence in which the chapters are arranged is of no special importance. The reader may elect to read the chapters in any order which he thinks is suited to his own special needs. In fact, you may unconventionally read the last chapter first, progressing backward to the front of the volume, and do just as well as one who conventionally reads chapter one first, progressing forward to the last.

J. J. V.

STUDY AND LIKE IT

CHAPTER I

The Profession of Studying

There are two classes of failures among college students. First there are those who cannot fulfill the minimum requirements set by the college and are forced to withdraw before the completion of the course. But there is another class of failures which is not quite so obvious—students who have fulfilled the minimum requirements and obtained their degrees, but who must candidly admit that their achievements have been far below the possibilities of their talent and opportunities.

UNRECORDED FAILURES

A diploma is not necessarily evidence of a successful college career. For diplomas are awarded even to those who have done nothing but mediocre work. No student can justly consider his four years at college a success unless he has derived from these years of educational opportunities a result which is commensurate with his native talent and ability. At least it is true that after four years of college work, there should be a marked and visible acquisition of learning. If this is absent, you have failed. Too many college graduates, in the reflective years of later life, look back upon the opportunities of college with wistful regret. For they are forced to acknowledge that their four years at college have not produced any solid intellectual achievements, that in the matter of intellectual taste, culture and sound scholarship their four years at college have been disappointingly empty and barren. In a word, there are too many unrecorded failures.

WHY STUDENTS FAIL

Students sometimes fail because they begin their college work with an inadequate background or with an insufficient preparation. Sometimes it is the intrusion of extraneous interests or a willful neglect of study. Seldom does a college student fail because of an outright insufficiency of natural talent. Almost any student who has done fairly good work in high school and who is willing to study can complete a general college course with a fair degree of success.

In my opinion college failures are to be attributed principally to two factors: an absence of any congenial interest in study and a lack of efficient study methods. The majority of students arrive at the college gate in September eager to make their college career a success. But few of them arrive with a genuine love of study or anything like a serious intellectual interest. Very frequently they come with an actual distaste for serious study. Moreover, many of them lack competence—not competence to learn, but competence in how to go about learning. They have heard many solemn warnings about their duty to study but have not received sufficient inspiration to love study. They have been chided for their lack of method, but no one has told them what the proper method is or even that there is a proper method. The purpose of this book is to inspire the student with a love of study and to teach him to take up the work of study in a competent, efficient manner.

THE PROFESSION OF STUDYING

You have been sent to college to learn. While one may learn by observation, experience, conversation and travel, a college man must do most of his learning by the more deliberate way of formal studying. Having entered college, studying is now your *profession*. For you studying is not an optional, occasional performance to be taken up now and then and worked into your daily life as it suits your convenience or pleasure. It is your duty, your principal occupation to which all other tasks and interests are to be subordinated. You have as much reason to be conscientious in the practice of your profession as a lawyer has in the practice of law or a physician in the practice of medicine. If you shun study, you are shirking your duty, playing the dishonorable role of a bluffer and abusing the confidence of those who may be responsible for your presence at college.

There is one thing about the profession of a student which is quite unique—he has no rivals who can deprive him of the fruit of his endeavors. One businessman may outwit another and steal his trade, but in your life as a professional student no one is your rival in the sense of being able to deprive you of the solid achievements of your labor. There are, of course, competition and rivalry among students, even competition and rivalry deliberately planned. But scholastic competition never defeats a student or robs him of the fruits of learning. Suppose you enter a contest for the best English essay and produce what, under the circumstances, is the best piece of literature which you are able to produce. Your roommate is awarded the medal and you arrive in seventh place. What of it? You have learned something of the subject, increased your vocabulary and improved your style of writing. These are your personal rewards which neither your roommate nor the president of the college can take from you. Your roommate's success takes nothing away from you. A student's true rewards are not medals, or honors, or even degrees. They are knowledge and intellectual proficiency. You are following a happy profession in which no rival's success endangers your own.

SELF-IMPOSED MEDIOCRITY

Daily contacts with your professors, instructors and fellow students will often make you keenly aware that you are surrounded by many who are your intellectual superiors. This should not be a depressing experience. If you recognize anyone as your intellectual superior, remember that he is your superior not so much by reason of circumstances or talent, but because he has studied more than you. Once your professor of mathematics, for instance, knew no more about the subject than you do now. He must have come into possession of that knowledge by studying. You must come into possession of knowledge the same way. We learn things by studying. Other things being equal, a superior student is a superior man. You may shun the labor of study, but if you do you are self-condemned to intellectual mediocrity.

LABOR OF STUDY

I employ the term "labor of study" deliberately. Studying *is* labor. How often we regretfully confess our ignorance of things which we would really like to know. How many exceptionally gifted minds there are which remain in a perpetual state of superficiality and comparative ignorance. If we could only exchange the desire of knowledge for knowledge by some facile process, ignorance would almost vanish from the earth. It is the labor of learning that too frequently stands between one's desire of learning and his actual possession of it. Somewhere in man's makeup there is a persistent aversion to effort, both physical and mental. There is no way to slay this enemy of enlightenment once and for all and get it out of the way forever. It keeps intruding upon us from day to day. Some days there is less, some days there is more. There is only one thing to do—to whip it every time it intrudes and be prepared to whip it again when it returns tomorrow. Genuine scholarship has more to fear from mental inertia than from a lack of talent. Intellectual sloth sterilizes our best desires. If one is to learn he must toil. Knowledge is transmuted mental labor.

But if studying is labor, it does not necessarily follow that it must be a distasteful occupation. One may work hard and enjoy it. Too many students regard studying as housewives look forward to the regular Monday washing—as a gloomy, dreary task that must be borne with heroic fortitude. The idea that studying day after day must be a monotonous, dreary performance is dead wrong. Studying can be one of the most delightful and enjoyable activities of life. For some people it actually is. When you study you are engaged in a process of discovery, the discovery of truth. Every hour of serious study terminates with additional knowledge. It opens the mind successively and progressively upon newer and newer fields of knowledge. It is unlocking door after door in a never-ending series of chambers, each with revelations of its own, each with vistas unsuspected before. It is an adventure in thinking which can be as exhilarating as an exploration in a strange and unexplored land. Study is toil, but a zestful toil animated by the joy of intellectual discovery.

MOTIVES

Since studying is labor, there must be some motive to undertake the effort. Most college students are motivated, in a general way, by a desire to equip themselves for a profitable position in the business or professional world. This desire is usually the reason why they are in college, in the first place. But here and there, and in addition to this general motive, there are other motives which operate most effectively. Some students, for instance, will study because they fear the chagrin of flunking, others because they attach a certain prestige to a degree and others because "they have to," etc. Any motive that makes one study is better than none. Since one must make a living after college days are finished, a general college course should have the benefit of practical utility. But I do not believe that a student should make utility, i.e., the utility of pecuniary profit, the sole motive of studying. A candid appreciation of art and literature, a knowledge of philosophy, history, astronomy, geology and many other subjects enlarge the mind and heart and help to make life worth living. Merely being alive is not living. Utility aspects of college education should be justly respected but should not be sought to the exclusion of cultural aspects. Some things are to be studied, therefore, simply because they are worth studying. I believe that a plain, intellectual curiosity and eagerness to learn for the sake of learning is the most sustaining motive of all, and excels all others in giving zest and joy to the profession of study.

GETTING STARTED

Now that you are in college get settled as quickly as possible and then get down to work without delay. Sometimes a student makes an initial error in consuming too much time grooving himself to his new surroundings. It is a period of transition too often marked by confusion and inefficiency. Certain preliminary matters, such as room and board, the purchase of books and supplies, meeting new acquaintances, etc., must be attended to and make a definite demand upon your time. Whatever preliminary arrangements demand immediate attention, settle definitely and promptly with the minimum expenditure of time. But there are many incidental matters which can be ignored for the present and which can be taken care of incidentally, as time goes on. Many students start their college course spinning about for four or five weeks in a state of mild confusion before they finally "get set." In the meantime examinations appear on the schedule before students have done any actually serious work. This is a great waste. Plunge yourself into your work at once.

IMPORTANT PERIOD

Remember that you are going to spend *four years* at college. Four years are a considerable fraction of any man's life, and four years at college are a very important fraction. Make up your mind now that they are going to be four "full years." These years are brief, but in opportunities for learning and development they will never be duplicated. I know a gardener who has a small truck farm and is making a comfortable living on four acres of ground. He makes every acre count. He is out with his plow the first open day in spring and sticks to the job till the approach of winter. Work your four years of college as this man works his four acres of ground. Start the work early, exactly with the first day of class, continue through and do not relax your efforts until the last. Every day must count.

Although you cannot realize it so vividly now, the four years you spend at college will form a most unique period of your life. Some day you will be looking back upon these years in retrospect. This retrospective glance in later life will yield no satisfaction if you are forced to recognize them as years that have been lean and barren. Wasted opportunities are always an affliction to remember.

Suggestions

1. Have you ever thought of studying as a professional duty? Is such an attitude unreal, impossible or too pretentious?
2. Do you really enjoy studying or is it just a mercenary task?
3. Do students generally consider "intellectual culture" as a conventional sham or as an ideal which is not meant to be taken seriously?
4. Are there any subjects which you would like to study but which are not taught in your college? In your opinion why are these subjects disregarded in the curriculum?
5. There may be certain subjects which you have taken without any perceptible degree of profit or personal satisfaction, or without having understood them. Analyze the cause of this failure. Was it due to the difficulty of the matter, lack of interest, failure to study or the incompetent manner in which the subject was taught?
6. What are the factors which really hinder you from getting down to serious work? Keep these in mind and note whether they are adequately treated in the following chapters.

CHAPTER II

Professional Attitudes

Very often a student's success at college is conditioned by his mental attitudes toward his college, its curriculum, studying and his own ability. His attitudes in these matters can be so harmful and antagonistic that they seriously hinder, and sometimes actually frustrate, a successful college career.

STUDENT REFORMERS

All good men desire to make the world better. But there is an undesirable tendency in many American students to take themselves too seriously by imagining that they have a personal, mysterious destiny to reform the world. They are impatient to demolish existing conventions, institutions and the restraints of time-honored discipline. They are earnestly enthusiastic about recasting the entire world after their own ideas of how things ought to be. They are not content with contributing their share of thought and action to progress. They want immediate change, a quick, tumultuous change in nearly everything.

Now every thinking person realizes that there is much that is stupid and wrong in the world that needs to be changed. But if you are still in college, you may take for granted that you have very little knowledge of how the world has come into its present plight and understand very imperfectly the practical processes whereby it can be improved. In fact, the acquiring of this deeper knowledge of the world should be one of the reasons why you are in college. Never relinquish the honest, noble desire of making the world better. But modestly recognize that your idealism is still the idealism of a youth, idealism still untamed by practical experience and awaiting inevitable correction by more mature understanding. Do not set yourself up too early in life as a critic and reformer of everything around you. This applies especially to your attitude toward your college. For after all, your life at college is, for the present at least, your world.

YOUR ATTITUDE TOWARD YOUR COLLEGE

Strike a friendly, cooperative attitude toward your college. Colleges are not commercial institutions paying dividends or institutions where men and women serve a period of voluntary servitude. Your college exists for you, with no material profit to itself. It is a center of influence which is meant to impart intellectual, cultural and moral training to all who come within the sphere of its active influence. All of its expensive equipment—buildings, gymnasium, library, laboratories—have been purchased and placed at your disposal for your personal benefit. Its faculty of professors and instructors are usually men and women specially trained, competent and chosen out of many for their exceptional qualifications of learning and ability. It is a privilege to associate with them and to profit from their instruction and experience. In every college some system of discipline is necessary. Whatever policies of discipline your college has adopted, they are not a set of rules arbitrarily enacted to make life miserable. They are regulations which are the result of wisdom and long experience. You are merely benefiting yourself and promoting the general welfare of the student body when you submit to the disciplinary regulations which your college imposes. Think of your college with all its functions, departments, equipment, faculty and discipline as a friendly ally to help you onward to your own goal of enlightenment and self-improvement.

This is quite different from the critical, rebellious attitude which students sometimes assume. In nearly every student body there is a sprinkling of chronic malcontents or "professional knockers" who discover that everything is wrong. No institution, of course, is perfect, and there may be things about your college which you are inclined to criticize. If your criticism is just, there is usually a proper time and place to make it known to responsible officials of the college. Just or well-meant criticism, if properly proposed, is usually welcomed and may be a helpful contribution.

But when a student haughtily adopts the air and the role of a general archcritic, he develops an attitude that is definitely antagonistic to good scholastic work. For the mind works best in an atmosphere of peace and contentment. Moreover, the chronic, sullen critic is often blind and insensitive to the many valuable advantages which actually surround him. Since everything cannot be wrong, some things must be right, and the important question is: Are you utilizing to the maximum the opportunities for self-development which your college actually offers? If you are not, you are more to blame than the college trustees.

It is not so much how your college ranks with other colleges in size, reputation or model equipment, but how *you* rank in regard to utilizing the advantages which it actually offers. For instance, there may be students who justly criticize the limitations of the college library but who do not avail themselves even of its limited offering. One might profit handsomely by reading the books that *are* there. Why should one spurn a few books because there are not more to read? It thus turns out that one may read nothing because he cannot read much, very similar to a hungry man refusing a plate of ham and eggs because he has not been invited to a six-course banquet.

TASTES

Some of the branches of study which you will be obliged to take at college will certainly not be to your personal liking or "taste"—perhaps mathematics, philosophy or poetry. This is to be expected. Even in the matter of intellectual pursuits, nearly everyone has his peculiar interests and particular aversions. One can hardly live and think without developing certain more or less well-defined intellectual interests which in the course of time begin to seem natural. I maintain, however, that no man is born with a taste for anything, but he *is* born hungry. What is ordinarily called a taste for this or that is merely one of a thousand potential aptitudes which has been developed by study and deliberation, modified by one's individual talents and sometimes favored by accidental circumstances. Tastes are largely our own creations. This being true, do not excuse your failures or palliate your mediocrity by comfortably assuming that you have no taste for this or that subject. If you have no taste, it may be your business to develop one, or it may be possible and desirable to learn the subject without one.

Moreover, it is a mistake to judge the importance or the value of any given branch solely on the basis of whether it is tasteful or distasteful. Every subject taught at college has its value and purpose. No knowledge is profitless. But it is true that students are often insensitive and ignorant of the broader values and especially of the cultural advantages of many things which they are obliged to study. Take poetry, for instance. The fact that you *like* poetry or not is no sensible criterion by which to decide whether you *ought* to study it. To the student's frequent question of "What's the use?"—which is a proper and intelligent question to ask—it is sometimes difficult to give an answer which fully convinces him. The use and value of some things cannot be fully realized, sometimes not realized at all, without experience. A poetic appreciation, for example, is not an innocent educational delicacy, as some are prone to regard it. It is a serious, important requisite for a truly educated man. Without poetic appreciation you may be a wise man but certainly a less cultured one. And if I assure you now that a knowledge and appreciation of poetry will make you a better writer, a more persuasive speaker, a more effective teacher, a more delightful conversationalist and that it will sweeten many an hour of your earthly existence, are you inclined to regard this assurance with skepticism or contradiction? Yet such *are* the tangible utilities of poetry. Should you allow a youthful aversion to poetry to prevail so that this subject is omitted or seriously neglected, you are shortchanging yourself and sacrificing some valuable advantages to your lasting hurt.

Sometime what one calls a taste or a distaste is merely a whim or a prejudice. A truly wise man candidly admits whatever whims or prejudices afflict him, but he does not allow them to sway and determine his judgment when issues of importance are at stake.

It is true, as I shall point out in another chapter, that an interest in a subject is a great advantage in learning it and that interests can be deliberately cultivated. Yet it is folly even to expect that interest or natural taste will rise to the student's assistance where there is almost complete ignorance. Very few people today, even educated people, have any intellectual interest in astronomy, although it used to be taught in high schools, for the simple reason that there is an almost universal illiteracy in the subject. One must first crack the ice by expelling his original ignorance. Intellectual interests and tastes will naturally follow.

So cultivate a wholesome appreciation for the value of all the branches of the curriculum, regardless of your personal tastes. None of them is useless. If you don't like mathematics, what of it? Tighten up your belt and study it anyway.

THE CULT OF THE EASY

Some of the subjects which appear in your curriculum will be hard. This is not mysterious and it should not intimidate you. Some subjects are difficult because of their nature. They deal with the abstract and the intricate and no one can make them otherwise. Thus chemistry is naturally more difficult than geography. Other subjects may owe their difficulty, at least in part, to the fact that the student meets them in college in a state of general unpreparedness. Plunged for the first time into the problems of logic, you find yourself at once in a strange and unfamiliar field unlike anything which you have ever studied. Some of its difficulties are merely due to the fact that you must begin it without the benefit of any previous preparation. Most beginnings are faltering and difficult. It is otherwise with college mathematics. In this field you have the decided advantage of a familiarity with the general nature of the subject and of some previous knowledge and training which will assist you to make the start. You are not a raw recruit. Other things being equal, you may expect logic to be more difficult than mathematics. Finally, almost any branch which requires serious study will be difficult to some students merely because they have never learned to study. The only available remedy for them is to learn how to study and like it.

Man's deep and incurable aversion to mental labor readily conditions him to accept the facile notion that everything worthy to be learned can be made easy. On every hand, there is evidence of the modern cult of "easy learning," with its promises of shortcuts, simple methods and quick results. How significant it is that Ernest Dimnet's *French Grammar Made Clear* has been repeatedly misquoted as *French Grammar Made Easy.** Before me is a magazine which advertises, *Learn Spanish in Twenty Easy Lessons.* Another one advertises, *Learn to Play the Piano in Twelve Lessons.* The tone of other advertisements conveys the impression that anyone can quickly and easily learn law, banking, or accounting by merely reading a few simple, graded books. Energetic textbook writers are in close pursuit of the facile adwriters, for they are publishing simple grammars like *Latin the Easy Way.* The cult of easy learning has won friends even in certain educational circles where there seems to be a general agreement that good pedagogy consists in finding the easiest method and convincing the students that learning is a "cinch." It is little wonder that soft-fibered students are trekking to college in search of snap courses and easy professors and are quite averse to getting down to the hard work of thinking.

If you are a student of average ability you should be able to see through the sham of the promise of knowledge without effort. There are many things which cannot be made easy because they are difficult. No textbook writer is clever enough to charm away the intricacies of Latin grammar. Your instructor in trigonometry is a magician if he can transmute the difficulty of his subject into the happy simplicity of Aesop's fables. Having taught logic for about eighteen years, I have never yet told my pupils that it is easy. I know it is not.

The cultists of the easy know this, too, but they seem willing to sacrifice sincerity for what is sometimes called "psychology." This brand of psychology assumes that to tell a student frankly that the matter before him is difficult and that he must study hard to learn it might unnerve him for the task. This is evidently an appeal *from* the truth and *to* a false mental dread which is supposed to lurk in the mind of the student. The right psychology is to admit the truth, appeal to the right motives and point out efficient methods of study.

So I say to the reader of this book that you may as well learn now to take the bitter with the sweet and that some of your subjects will require

---

*Cf. Ernest Dimnet, *The Art of Thinking* (New York: Simon & Schuster, Inc.), p. 64.

hard work. I do not say that subjects which are difficult are for that reason important. But it is certainly true that some important subjects are difficult. After all, you have come to college for an education, and no one has acquired an education in pleasant, easy doses. An athlete is not trained by lying in bed or playing croquet. To elect a curriculum composed of snap courses or to neglect the study of important subjects because they are difficult is a good way to make yourself an intellectual starveling.

If you are a student of average ability and if you are not mentally indolent, your dread of any course that is hard is likely nothing more than an unfounded mistrust of your own ability, easily accounted for, which you may safely disregard. You may expect to do quite well in any subject since thousands of other students with less intelligence than yours have passed through the same course with excellent results. Perseverance, as well as brilliance, has its victories.

The good "psychologists" who preach the doctrine of easy and pleasant methods apparently assume that you identify hard work with drudgery. They should tell you that such an identification is erroneous. A thing may be difficult yet quite interesting. Indeed, intelligent people really enjoy the mystery and intrigue of problems which do not yield their solutions too readily. The obvious is often shorn of interest. Chess is more absorbing than checkers, though more difficult. Croquet is less interesting than baseball, though more simple. So the chances are that logic will be more interesting to you than geography. Normally alert people easily become fascinated with studies which are intricate enough to offer their minds a challenge. It is quite probable, then, that the difficult subjects of your curriculum will in the course of time become your favorites.

NATURE'S EXCEPTION

It is possible that you possess some natural gifts and aptitudes which qualify you better for one subject than for another, although what is commonly called a special "talent" is often merely a proficiency acquired by continuous study and application and quite within the reach of almost everyone. Do not cozen the idea that you are mysteriously circumscribed by destiny, or that you are some rare product of nature especially "cut out" for certain things. It is a facile, uncritical notion that can be easily turned into a plausible excuse for one's own culpable deficiencies and failures. A student fails in logic and writes home that he is not cut out for philosophy. It may be that he has no interest in philosophy or that he is too lazy to study it. But to say that he is not cut out for philosophy seems to me to be an erroneous explanation bordering upon the ludicrous.

Man's worst illusions nest in his indolence and vanity. You are probably not cut out for anything because you are capable, with proper interest and study, to learn almost anything. There may be exceptions, but do not get into the habit of thinking that you are one of nature's exceptions.

STUDY ADVENTUROUSLY

Start any subject hopefully with fine gusto and the happy air of an adventurer. Say to yourself "I don't know what it is about, but I will find out, and there will be something there that will interest and profit me."

Experienced travelers often say that there are interesting things to see almost everywhere they happen to go. One year I made a deliberate experiment. I was on a train going west to the coast. I got out a railroad map and followed the long black line which marked my course across the continent. Off the main road on which I was traveling I noticed the town of Carson City, Neveda. I knew nothing of Carson City except that it was the capital of the state, nothing of its history and nobody among its inhabitants. I just said to myself, "I'll interrupt my journey at the next stop and take a bus to Carson City. There should be something interesting in this secluded place." Well, it was a most delightful experience. I could write a long account of the interesting things and people in and around Carson City, Nevada. And here I almost passed it up because I had heard so much about San Francisco and Los Angeles. Thus my suspicion was confirmed that there is something interesting almost in any place you choose to go, no matter how remote or little heard of it is. But you must have energy and determination enough to move out of your tracks and go to see it. On the same principle I am going to take a plane some day and suddenly alight in Kokomo, Indiana. If you want to get the most out of travel, just travel—adventurously, hopefully. Places don't come to you. You must go to places.

Study the same way. Wade into your subject with the will and bearing of an adventurer, anticipating a great pleasure without knowing what it may be, but convinced that it will be there. Such an adventurous approach brings you to your subject eager and alert—a pretty good springboard to success. It liberates you at once from the mental encumbrances of dread, prejudice and hopeless fear which often take the wind out of a student before he gets started.

Suggestions

1. Are there some things about your college which you do not like? Any nuisances which should be abated? Any genuine hindrances to

eliminate? How would you bring these matters to the attention of the proper authorities?

2. Do you think that you have any special tastes or any special talent for a particular subject? Any special prejudice or lack of competence? How do you account for these?
3. Do you think that you are especially cut out for anything? Why?
4. Have you ever had the experience of beginning a course with a strong dislike for the subject and arriving at the end with a genuine interest in it? What caused the change of attitude? What does this suggest?
5. Why do you think that astronomy and geology are so widely disregarded in our college curricula?
6. What are the *avowed* purposes of youth movements in some American colleges? What are the *real* purposes? What is the good of such movements? What are the dangers? Does "remote control" suggest anything to you?
7. Should a college magazine be edited and published independently of supervision by responsible college authorities?

CHAPTER III

Aids to Superficiality

Your aim as a student should always be sound scholarship. Take up a subject to *learn* it. If you do not intend to learn it, it is better to leave it alone, if you may. Of course, when I say "learn a subject," I am not referring to complete mastery, which sometimes requires years to achieve. I mean your studying a subject should in every case terminate with some ponderable acquisition, some definite competence in the matter. This is a result quite removed from a "smattering" acquaintance. The smatter method is often noticeable, if not scandalous, in the field of foreign languages. There is little use taking up a language unless you intend to terminate the course with a fair ability to read the language and with a little facility at easy conversation. It is quite possible to spend four years at college going through the motions of studying and to remain lightly on the surface of everything with nothing solidly learned. The end result is a light sophistication or pedantry, which is one of the more attractive forms of illiteracy, purchased at great cost but adding little to the mind except the vice of vanity. Subjects of study, then, are to be solidly and competently learned, not merely "taken."

There are several influences which invite one to superficiality. They are hazards to sound scholarship which you should be able to recognize in order to defend yourself against them. Some of them originate in the student himself, others in educational policies which may be followed in certain colleges.

CREDIT CHASERS

There is an inclination among students to misinterpret the value and purpose of credits. Colleges give credits for subjects taken and require a certain number of earned credits for graduation. Whatever the merits of the present credit system may be, any college must establish a definite minimum standard for graduation which must ultimately assume some concrete form and which must be applied with some kind of exactness approaching rigidity. The credit system is merely a convenient way of applying what is generally believed to be a fair standard of college work. So you must earn a certain number of credits before a diploma is awarded.

This is merely a policy of administration and should not induce you to take up subjects for the sole purpose of accumulating credits. Colleges which permit a too liberal elective system are a happy hunting ground for a good credit chaser. He chooses subjects that are easy, prefers courses taught by easy professors and manages to accumulate the required number of credits with the minimum amount of mental exertion. But such a selection results in little correlation between the various subjects taken and little coordination of his college work to his ultimate purposes. His college course is made up of unrelated patches and lacks the value and solidity of a well-balanced unit.

The correct way is to choose your course with a definite plan in view. Certain subjects are so related that they mutually clarify and complete one another with the result of a balanced pattern. Obviously there is an advantage to combining such subjects, taking them either simultaneously or successively. Other subjects may be chosen because they are more suitably geared to your ultimate objectives. One expecting to enter the field of journalism, for instance, would have good reason for studying sociology or for specializing in history, with less emphasis on mathematics. Other subjects are necessary for the rounded development of any cultured, educated person, regardless of the specific avocation which he may have in view. In every college there are faculty advisors who will assist you in planning your course.

Choose your course wisely and let the credits take care of themselves. Credits will then be the result of your choice but not the motive.

NOVELTY SEEKERS

Disappointment and superficiality are often the only rewards to seekers of novelty in education. The novelty search is illustrated by students who take up a course merely to see what it is like. They have had a taste of Latin and now, without any intention of learning it, they are anxious to see what French is like. Or they go in for sociology not because they have any enlightened interest in the subject or any particular use for it, but because they have never had it before. Sometimes it takes the form of choosing a subject principally for the purpose of trying out a professor who has the reputation of being an entertaining lecturer. Here it is not so much a desire to sample the course as to sample the professor, for they have never had him before. Occasionally a student is intrigued into taking a subject by the catchy, snappy title with which some versatile professor has labeled his course. College catalogues sometimes reveal titles of courses which suggest a degree of charlatanry very similar to the trick of merchants who intrigue the public into buying an old article by displaying it in a bright new wrapper.

There is in everyone, especially in youth, a certain restlessness, a desire for change and a yearning to try the new, which is not to be deplored or discouraged. But the love of novelty and change should be restrained. It should not prevail to set at naught the sound principle that "to learn one thing well is better than to learn several things superficially." In learning there is no substitute for thoroughness. Louis is a fairly bright boy, has completed his high school work with one year of French and goes off to college. He drops his French, which has been quite well begun, to sample a year of Spanish. Now he is wondering what German is like. He may have a talent and an interest in languages, but he has made a mistake by not continuing his French through college. With two or three additional years of French he might have gained a firm grip on this language which would have served him through life. As it is, being a novelty seeker he will probably leave college with a superficial knowledge of three foreign languages without knowing any one of them well. When you once get a start in a subject, carry through to a point of proficiency. You cannot know everything, but there is nothing to prevent you from learning a few things well.

TOO MANY SUBJECTS

Students sometimes raise the complaint that they are forced to take too many subjects simultaneously. I believe the complaint is sometimes justified. The simultaneous pursuit of eight different subjects, for instance, is a cheap educational policy ruinous of sound scholarship. This is scattering attention over too many fields at one time. Two factors are involved here—time and the psychic element of active interest. To study a subject well means enlisting a high interest in it and putting in many hours of continuous study. You cannot be actively and continuously interested in more than five or six branches of knowledge at one time. Interest should flow at high tide, and when it does it crowds on other interests. At any rate, there is a limit to time and six hours a week spent in studying mathematics leaves fewer hours for studying other subjects. In the work of studying, one may reach a saturation point. After all, there is a limit to the supply of the possible number of one's active interests and a limit to the supply of time which one can give to study. So if you are driving ahead with a half a dozen subjects intently and more or less continuously, you are probably absorbing all the psychic power and all the time for study which an ordinary student possesses.

If you find that you are forced, by some atrocious policy prevailing in your college, to take more than a safe number of courses at any one given time, there is only one thing to do to protect yourself—concentrate on five or six which you deem more important and deliberately neglect the others as far as you may. You must determine not to be a superficial student. Colleges that permit too much of a spread are merely window dressing the student's curriculum and encouraging the popular trend toward superficial, showy scholarship.

ONE-HOUR-A-WEEK COURSES

Finally, all serious students come to realize sooner or later that learning a subject well requires a certain continuity of study and application. Too many long gaps between study periods and class periods are detrimental to the process of thorough learning. For good results, there must be a generous amount of concentrated study spread more or less evenly and smoothly over a given space of time. This space of time may be relatively brief, but there must be something like a continuous flow of effort while the effort lasts.

Thus it is easy to understand the weakness and waste of "one-hour-a-week" courses. Allowing for a few possible exceptions, a planned interval of a week between class periods is a pedagogical error and a wasteful arrangement which is seldom necessary. The matter taken in one class has too much time to cool off and is hard to warm up for the next class. A weekly spurt is merely pecking at the subject, a kind of a desultory, innocuous nibble.

The pedagogical justification of one-hour-a-week courses in college where practically the whole student body is in daily attendance is difficult to understand. If it is desirable to devote only a limited amount of time to the rudiments of geology, for instance, even this limited amount of time should be efficiently employed to achieve maximum results. If thirty-two lectures are to be devoted to a subject, why is it necessary to distribute them thinly over thirty-two weeks? The same number of lectures could be given with probably a greater amount of material covered in eight weeks with four lectures a week. Such an arrangement is more efficient, from the standpoint of sound scholarship, than spacing the classes with lean and lonesome intervals between them—a wasteful distribution of effort requiring additional repetition on the part of the instructor and alienating interest on the part of the student.

Admitting that there are a few exceptions, I believe that you may regard one-hour-a-week courses with justifiable suspicion.

Suggestions

1. Have you ever elected to take a course because you thought it was going to be easy? Because you considered it a kind of novelty? Because of the easy methods or the popularity of the instructor? Were you satisfied with the results?
2. Do you think that a student can carry eight subjects during any one semester and do efficient work? Judging from your own experience what is the chief hindrance in taking too many subjects?
3. Have you ever gotten much out of one-hour-a-week courses? How are such courses generally regarded by the students?
4. Could the teaching of such courses be effectively coordinated into fewer weeks with more class periods per week? Would you prefer such a concentration? In your opinion are the reasons for maintaining one-hour-a-week schedules administrative or pedagogical?
5. Would you favor condensing two-hour-a-week subjects to four hours per week, shortening the course period in proportion?

CHAPTER IV

Concentration

One may be mentally occupied without studying. Indeed, there is never a moment of the waking day when the mind is entirely vacant of thought. We are always, in our conscious moments, thinking about something. When the mind, however, is merely the scene of promiscuous, unrelated thoughts coming and going in capricious succession with little or no effort on the part of the thinker to direct their course or make them serve a purpose, the mind is "occupied," but only in the sense that it is not vacant. This is merely a state of mental passivity in which purposeless thoughts dominate the mind rather than the mind purposely dominating the thoughts. It is really intellectual idleness and the direct opposite of the process of studying.

WHAT IS STUDY?

At other times, however, the mind actively and resolutely directs its thinking toward a goal, e.g., when one is absorbed in the performance of some task like repairing an automobile, writing a letter, reading a novel or playing a game. In such cases thoughts are more or less systematically summoned, held to a regular course and consciously directed to an end. It is a controlled and purposeful mental action. The mind is really "employed," not merely "occupied." Yet this is not studying.

Such purposeful mental action becomes studying when it is undertaken for the immediate purpose of acquiring knowledge. Studying may be defined as the systematic application of the mind to given subject matter for the immediate purpose of understanding it. It is an aggressive state of mind wherein the intellectual powers are summoned *to attack*. The immediate objective of the attack is to learn something.

But to achieve this objective the attack must be a sustained effort of some intensity. In other words, the most essential factor of successful studying is controlled, continuous attention or concentration. Concentration is bringing the full attention and the various powers of the mind to bear continuously on a definite subject. How rarely does one really employ his full intellectual powers to their utmost capacity and hold them to the peak of their maximum performance continuously over a considerable length of time! If one did so frequently, the results might be astonishing. Your most serious problem as a student, then, is the problem of better concentration.

INEFFICIENCY OF POOR CONCENTRATION

Nothing reveals the full importance of this problem more clearly than to consider the appalling inefficiency of poor concentration. When you fail to concentrate properly you are introducing inefficiency on a grand scale by wasting time and hampering comprehension. You may verify this statement by analyzing the way you sometimes listen to a lecture. The mind actually contacts the subject matter irregularly in a few desolatory spots. Between the moments of actual contact, several moments elapse in which your mind has wandered off to other matters which are irrelevant. It may easily happen that the "off attention" periods total as many minutes as the "attention" periods, in which case a fifty-minute lecture period has actually been reduced to twenty-five minutes. Thus fifty minutes are consumed in doing the work of twenty-five.

Besides being a great waste of time, such sporadic attention impairs your actual understanding of the matter treated. When the mind is now at attention, let us say for three minutes, the matter treated during this brief period may be quite well understood. But there follows a period of inattention lasting say two minutes. Then the mind returns to the subject of the lecture. But in the meantime the thought of the lecture has advanced, and you have to hook on at that point. Here is the difficulty. The understanding of the matter under treatment at this particular point may require the understanding of the matter which you have just missed. Consequently, you have difficulty in making the new contact, and when it is made it is made imperfectly. The more spotty the attention, the more imperfect is the general understanding of the lecture. No wonder you leave the lecture room with a sense of little accomplished. This, of course, applies also to reading and periods of private study.

Once you understand clearly that poor concentration is a waste of time and a hindrance to understanding, you have taken the first step toward its improvement.

AIDS TO CONCENTRATION

As a student you will continue to labor under a serious handicap unless you acquire a fair degree of concentration power. Something, therefore, must be done. The following suggestions for improving the habit of concentration are largely the result of my own experience and are offered for what they are worth. Not all of them are of equal value. You may add to them or modify them on the basis of your own experience.

1. Concentration is a mental *habit* and like any good habit requires an individual impulse of the will to initiate and sustain it. Resolve then to be a student who is good at concentration. Keep that resolution before your mind whenever you read, study or listen to a lecture. From now on you are done with creeping along, enfeebled by habits of poor concentration. Whatever may be your present habits of mental errancy, these are to end and the start is to be made now. Think of yourself from now on as one who has set a goal—the mental habit of concentration.

2. Set this resolution into action at once, i.e., the first time you apply yourself to any form of study, whether it be listening to a lecture, reading or studying a textbook. If you have a mathematics lesson to study tonight, make this a test case and make your resolution yield its first fruit. Tasting the first fruit of a good resolution is an encouraging and a comforting experience.

3. Attack each period of study with a hard, vigorous initiative. Don't waste time getting started. Step into your stride with a minimum of introductory effort. When one starts to study there is usually an initial period of warming up. There is usually some reluctance in starting. We read the first paragraphs rather slowly and painfully and wonder if we had not better take up something else. These initial deterrents are to be more or less expected. Only rarely can one bring full powers of his mind into instant action by one clean thrust like a diver who spears the water with a single plunge. Some initial difficulties may be usually expected, even patiently submitted to, but do not allow them to postpone the actual serious starting indefinitely. Dispatch them as quickly as possible and get on to the real business of earnest study with the least possible delay.

4. Be artful and resolute in handling distractions.. This is an important factor. Distractions are inevitable in the course of an ordinary lecture or study period. They cannot all be handled alike. They must be treated in the manner suited to their kind.

There are many petty distractions which, with a little will power, can be quietly ignored: someone walking across the room, a whispered conversation, the honk of an automobile horn, the rattle of a train, etc. Nothing can be done about these except quietly to ignore them. Excellent concentration can be sustained in spite of them. To allow them to interrupt and turn the stream of attention betrays a lack of resolution and purpose.

There are, however, major distractions which cannot be treated so summarily: you are called to the telephone, a visitor calls, someone asks you a question, a door slams with a deafening report, a firetruck clangs down the street, etc. These are intrusions which cannot be snubbed by merely tightening your grip on your work. They must be attended to but with firm dispatch. If you are interrupted by someone asking a question, courtesy demands that you answer the question. But it would be wasteful to protract the answer into a chat. If you are suddenly disturbed by a noisy firetruck passing the house, your work must be interrupted for a moment, but there is no need to go to the window to see which way the truck is going. Squeeze the loss of time occasioned by such interruptions to the minimum, then promptly forget them as though they had never occurred and quietly resume your work.

Although such unavoidable interruptions are bad enough at all times, they are worse if they are allowed to provoke such emotional disturbances as anger, irritation or resentment. No one can study while he is growling to himself in a state of irascible resentment. Mental quietude is a valuable asset, especially to a student. It may help to recall, before beginning a period of study, that some interruptions may be normally expected, and when they occur take them with an air of pleasant good humor. Good humor and a pleasant disposition are soothing to the nerves, your own as well as others, and will save you from wasting good study time in useless fretting about things you cannot help.

But not all distractions are environmental. When study time is shared by vagrant, purposeless thoughts of yesterday and tomorrow, reveries and daydreaming, there is an end to serious concentration. Such dissipating trends of thought are very likely to intrude when things are quiet and you are quite free from any external distractions. Fortunately, distractions rising from your own mind are largely within your own control. Beginning to study with a hard, vigorous effort, as explained above, helps to check their appearance and to build up a mood of active resistance. But there is no mental prophylactic which will immunize one from these subjective disturbances. Sometimes nothing will save the day for good concentration except a stern will and resolution to exclude purposeless thoughts whenever and as often as they arise. The effective control of one's vagrant thoughts is a character trait which is only developed by repeated effort and the willingness to strive for it. To guard one's own thoughts strongly, inviting the thoughts that should be there and excluding those that should not, is will power and self-mastery in its most perfect form. The lack of such self-command may explain why the results of long years of study are often so disappointingly meager in spite of fine opportunities and even sincere desires. There is a character element, a moral problem, involved in sound learning which cannot be connived at.

Sometimes when you sit down to study, your mind is thronged with thoughts of *other* tasks which you ought to do or *other* things which you have forgotten to do in the course of the day. The mind is then a scene of rivalry between these extraneous tasks and the present work of study. There is a temptation to desert or to interrupt study for other things needing attention. Remembering that studying is your profession, never omit your customary period of study or seriously interrupt it for any other task, unless for one of superior importance which requires immediate attention. But ninety-nine percent of these tasks which bid for attention when you once get studying are not of this superior sort. Some of them may be important, but nearly all of them can wait. While I am writing these lines, I can think of a half a dozen things, some of them important, which ought to be done. But they all can wait and the writing will go on. The best remedy against these allurements to interrupt serious work once undertaken is a memo pad. If you happen to recall while studying that you should mail a letter, call for your laundry or deliver a message and are afraid of forgetting it, simply make a note of it on a writing pad and resolve to take care of it at a suitable time. Then definitely forget the task for the present. Thus the matter is quietly disposed of with practically no interruption in study.

5. Select a suitable place to study. This factor is connected with the one preceding. The place where most of your studying is done should be a place which permits or invites as few distractions as possible. If you live at home, arrange to have a room reserved to yourself where you can do your studying *unobserved by others* and where others will not intrude. Let others in the house know that they are not to disturb you while you are there, except for matters that are important. Trivial things can always wait. Remember that when you study you are at work.

If it is impossible to have such an arrangement, the next best thing is a quiet corner which is more or less out of the way and which will yield, at least, a little privacy and freedom from ordinary interruption. Unfortunately, the modern way of building a house, turning the entire lower floor into one large chamber, is not an arrangement favoring privacy. A caller at the front door is a disturbance to the whole house, and a conversation or a radio playing in one corner is audible throughout the house. This, of course, is an annoyance for a student who wants a place where he can be by himself. Do the best you can under the circumstances. The kitchen table may often be suitable. If so, do not hesitate to turn the kitchen into a study. Almost any place is good enough if it affords quiet and seclusion. The school library is often a desirable study place. Make the maximum use of it if your home conditions are irreconcilable to serious studying. Having selected the most suitable place for study, dedicate it exclusively, if possible, to that purpose so that it becomes the place where you do all your customary studying and where nothing else but that is done. In time the place will become happily associated in your mind with study. Gradually it will become supplied with the necessary little equipment which a student needs, and it will be inviting because of its convenience. Moreover, the memories of peace and serious thought habitually associated with the place will surround it with a studious atmosphere positively conducive to concentration.

6. Keep your desk neat. All books, papers and miscellaneous objects not needed in the business of studying or unrelated to the subject of your present study should be kept out of sight. A disorderly desk littered with an assortment of objects irrelevant to study is a perfect nest of distractions. However, a vase of flowers or a beautiful picture may give pleasure without distracting the mind when one pauses to rest the eyes for a moment of mental relaxation. You may also find it advantageous to arrange your desk, if possible, so that you have a window view commanding a scene of natural beauty, such as a lawn, tree or field. Street scenes, however, afford little rest either to the eyes or to the nerves.

7. Select the most suitable time for study. As you progress in the art of concentration, you will gradually discover that certain periods of the day are more favorable for study than others. The particular value of certain periods is often dependent upon the physical condition of the body. Some people find that their efficiency is at a low ebb about four o'clock in the afternoon. If one has been working hard all day, he may expect some physical and mental fatigue to appear at this time. Your own experience will reveal what periods of the day are marked by low mental efficiency. Such periods should then be regularly reserved for other necessary tasks unrelated to study—shopping, visiting, exercising, etc. If you are dead tired after lunch, rest awhile and relax completely. A brief siesta of even twenty minutes, followed by a splash of cold water, may be quite sufficient to tone yourself up for the afternoon session. Do not try to study immediately after a full meal. This is the time to relax.

If home conditions are generally unfavorable to seclusion, study the situation to asertain what periods are relatively quiet and turn them to your best advantage. There may be whole days when you will be left to yourself. Anticipate these days, earmark them for study and employ them to your maximum profit.

8. Study under planned pressure. This may be accomplished by marking out definite goals to be reached within a given time and making a vigorous effort to reach them within the time limit set. For instance, if you have a term paper to write, plan to spend four or five hours at research reading, one hour arranging your notes and elaborating a plan and three hours writing. Marshal your study periods like a general disposing his regiments and expect definite results from given periods of

study. Naturally the work actually accomplished will not always correspond exactly with the amount of work originally planned and expected, but in most instances the discrepancy will not be great.

Every student has had the pleasant and assuring experience of doing an unexpected amount of good work laboring under pressure of time. You have your chemistry experiments, for instance, to write up and hand in on a certain day. You have postponed starting the work until the evening before the assignment is due. With three or four hours of steady application, without losing a minute, you finish the assignment which otherwise would have consumed two or three times this amount of time and are gratified with the results. Such experiences are frequent enough in a student's career to convince him of what can be done when he is working "full force." I am not, of course, intimating that a student should postpone work until the last minute in order to derive the benefit of working under pressure, nor am I an advocate of continuous, hard-pressure study at all times. Such a discipline, if adopted as a general policy, would work disastrously against the student in the long run. But a mild form of pressure demanding definite results of yourself for different periods of work is one way to eliminate a waste of time and to secure a high degree of concentration while at work.

9. There are certain aids and hindrances to concentration which may be classified as physical. As you progress in the profession of studying, you may discover many of these for yourself. Correct body posture should become a habit. While studying or listening to a lecture, the body should assume a posture that is natural and comfortable. A position which cramps and strains the body induces restlessness and premature fatigue. But reposing in a listless, lackadaisical position invites a languid mood which is not favorable to energetic thinking. A soft, deeply upholstered chair is not the best equipment for an energetic student. If you are working at a desk, sit erect in the chair so that your back rests solidly against the back of the chair and have the desk close to the body so that it offers a natural rest to the arms without requiring a crouching, stooping position. Sit up straight and close to the desk in a businesslike way, as you sit at the table to eat.

Students sometimes accustom themselves to little unnecessary, extraneous occupations during the study period which may be nothing more serious than innocent mannerisms. But do not allow yourself to become habituated, while studying, to nuisances—like cigarette smoking, eating candy, etc.—which divide attention and require innumerable interruptions of work.

Good physical tone is important for concentrated study. Sleepiness is often a problem. Drowsiness occurring early in the day or at any time when it cannot be attributed to work may be regarded as a temporary handicap, which a brief period of relaxation, a splash of cold water or a cool shower may easily remove.

10. Developing a permanent sustaining motive for the labor of studying is such an important factor contributing to concentration that the following chapter shall be exclusively reserved for its consideration.

Suggestions

1. Define "study." A good definition should distinguish studying from other kinds of mental employment.
2. From your own experience, can you give a practical example of how a lack of concentration has hindered comprehension and entailed a great loss of time?
3. Make a list of various distractions which you encounter while studying. Which ones are environmental? Which ones subjective? Draw up a plan or a practical policy of handling them.
4. What is your usual study place? Is it ideal? Is it the best possible under your present circumstances?
5. Is your home life conducive or detrimental to study? Make a careful survey of it with the purpose of improving it and making it as nearly ideal for a place to study as your circumstances permit.
6. Is there any special advantage or disadvantage to studying out-of-doors?

CHAPTER V

Motives

There are people with superior intellectual gifts who go idling through life with nothing thoroughly learned and with no solid intellectual achievements. They may have read voraciously and widely, may have passed through the opportunities of a college course and found no difficulty securing a degree. Yet in spite of talent, industry and opportunity, they remain lightly on the surface of everything they have touched, with nothing thoroughly learned, entirely lacking the perspective, depth and precision which mark a true scholar. They have not really educated themselves. They have merely wrapped themselves up in a cloak of pedantry. What a sharp contrast they make with certain others who have risen to marked intellectual attainments in spite of mediocre talent and relatively inferior opportunities! These dilettantes deserve to be counted as real casualties because their actual achievements are so slight in proportion to their superior talents and opportunities. They represent a tremendous capital which, considering the small returns, is a miserable waste. Underlying such failures is the lack of any serious, noble purpose. Put a definite, vivid purpose before you, and your efforts and resources of talent, whatever they may be, will be massed and thrown into your work with singular force and efficiency. Without such a purpose, in spite of your talents, opportunities and four years at college, you are foredoomed to mediocrity.

WISH VS. PURPOSE

Do not mistake a wish for a purpose. A wish is the mind beholding something as agreeable and desirable to possess or experience. Think of a comprehensive knowledge of history. Does this appeal to you as something that would be worthwhile to possess? Does your mind revert at least occasionally to this matter and each time with a sense of agreeableness? Would you really like to have such knowledge? Such an attitude or condition of mind is a wish. A wish always centers upon a thing that is absent. The mind understands this absent thing as something of worth and value. This understanding kindles a glow of appreciation. There is the thought, not the intention, of possessing or experiencing it, and this thought awakens an agreeable reaction.

A wish may be faint or strong. It may be transient or permanent. It may even extend to things that are recognized as impossible—one might wish to fly like a bird, walk across the floor of the ocean or live forever. Usually, and with better sense, it extends to possible things, whether these be remote or proximate, whether quite difficult to achieve or easily within grasp.

The important thing to observe is that *a wish is idle*. It is attention to an object without intention. It achieves nothing. It regards a thing as desirable, but it does not set up this thing as a goal of endeavor and stirs no determination to move toward its acquisition. It does not say, "Get up and go." It is not even "hope," which is the attitude of frank expectation of possessing an absent good.

Making one forsake the repose of sloth and undertake the effort of concentrated study requires much more than the wish to learn. Many people live all their lives with fine wishes—they wish to be good writers, good speakers, good musicians, etc.—but there the matter ends. Nearly every ignoramus *wishes* to know history, but so long as his attitude toward history remains at the "goodwill" level, his ignorance continues. A little scrutiny of your own mind will reveal how numerous these sincere but unproductive "wishes" to know and to learn are. However, a wish, especially if more or less permanent and strong, has its value. It may make you discontented with your ignorance and incompetence and ripen into a full purpose or motive.

If you examine any one of your activities, like a trip to a distant city or studying a history lesson, you will discover that it is a series of steps undertaken *because* they lead up to some desired end or goal. This goal, whatever it be, is some absent good which has so claimed your attention that you not only regard it as something agreeable to possess, but *as something which you now actually become determined to possess*. It is still an absent good, still beyond your actual grasp, yet it is so present to the mind that it reacts and elicits a series of efforts directed to its actual attainment. Think of this absent good merely as the chosen goal of endeavor, and you may call it a *purpose*. Think of it under its dynamic aspect, i.e., as reacting upon you and causing you to move toward its attainment, and you may call it a *motive* or an *incentive*. Purpose and motive are merely two sides of one and the same thing, viz., the distant good which you have decided to possess.

But we need not be so technical and precise. I was merely going to say that a motive is much different from a mere wish. A wish is inactive and does not accomplish. A motive or incentive (call it purpose if you like) establishes something as a goal and sets you in motion toward its achievement. A motive is dynamic and operative. It goes places, turns things over and moves onward in the direction of the contemplated good.

We are now ready to apply these reflections to your profession as a student. No one sits down to the task of studying without a motive. If studying and reading are to be done efficiently, with massed concentration, and carried continuously over a long period of time, the moving incentive must be strong and lasting. It must be strong enough to counterbalance one's natural tendency to indolence and to outbid rival motives which are sure to assert themselves. It must be lasting in the sense that it carries over from day to day, for studying is not an occasional occupation, but a continuous pursuit of months and years. An ephemeral incentive, the kind that is unsteady and short-lived, may be good enough while it lasts, but it produces nothing but sporadic attempts to study. Studying "in spurts" is one method to avoid.

MOTIVES VARY

Consider how the same subject matter may be diligently studied by different individuals, each compelled by varying incentives. Take history, for example. There is the student who is hard at work merely to avert the chagrin and inconvenience of flunking. He is working to avoid impending disaster. To a certain degree this motive operates at times on nearly all students. Another one studies because he is alertly conscious that he needs credit in history to obtain his degree. Studying history is simply the practical thing to do. Another applies himself to the task because he is convinced that putting in so many hours of study each day is his duty. He is motivated by a sense of duty. Another may study to maintain his class standing. He is motivated by the desire for recognition and prestige. But another is hard at work on his history to satisfy his interest in the subject, for the satisfaction of an intellectual interest can be a delightful and sustaining incentive. We can imagine that a writer who contemplates producing an historical drama may spend many serious hours studying history in order to provide himself with necessary general information and historical background. A lecturer in economics may study the same subject because he is searching for material to confirm or refute a certain economic theory, such as the "economic determination of history." Your own history professor may be busy studying history tonight in order to perfect his own course and improve his methods of classroom treatment. Here we have eight people studying history, each moved by a different purpose.

These examples also illustrate how different motives may dovetail and become interrelated in the mind of one individual. Seldom is one inspired to study by one single motive to the exclusion of all others.

Usually there are several motives at work which integrate to form a team with one motive in the lead and the others collaborating. A particular student may be moved to sustained study chiefly by the incentive of class honors and personal distinction, but there may be other motives, as a candid interest in the subject and the necessity of getting a diploma, which contribute valuable support, although standing somewhat in the background.

The full force which induces you to take up the work of study will depend on the *number of motives* which are active. Three motives are better than one. It will also depend on the *strength and vitality of each.* Two strong motives are better than two weak ones. Some incentives are so feeble that they elicit only a faint effort, while others are strong enough to command a vigorous assault. It will also depend upon the *quality of permanence.* Studying history to pass an examination may be a powerful incentive while it lasts. But it does not last long. Such a student will promptly cease to study history after the examination hazard is past. The goal he has set up is achieved, and once the goal is achieved the motive has vanished. Other incentives, like a genuine interest in the subject, are more permanent. Such an incentive wears well; in fact, it tends to entrench itself and will keep you studying more or less evenly and consistently, regardless of impending examinations.

MOTIVES AND CONCENTRATION

This question of purpose is related to concentration. Let us say that you do not hate studying, that your attitude toward the matter is really friendly. You do not lack goodwill. You would really like to study. In fact, you actually do study a great deal but seldom with any marked concentration and always with a remorseful sense of little or nothing accomplished. If this is your case, if you really want to study but find it difficult to concentrate, the reason for your difficulty may simply be that you have no strong purpose to do so. But this is no simple difficulty. Wishes and goodwill are not sufficient. This is another way of saying that studying must not only look good to you, but *very* good, so good, in fact, that you are induced to pour out streams of steady, controlled attention upon it, in spite of opposing obstacles and difficulties. You must approach the work of study with a strong purpose.

ANALYZING MOTIVES

"But how can I develop such a strong purpose?" There is no sleek, facile formula to offer for the development of such a purpose. There is no magic approach to the matter of learning. Yet some help may come from a candid analysis of your own career and experiences as a student. You have already done some studying, perhaps a great deal. Regardless of how you have succeeded, what are the motivating factors which make you set other things aside and get down to the work of serious study? Nearly every student may recognize the following motives:

1. *Utility.* By this I mean the practical value which one expects to derive from his knowledge in terms of making a living, securing employment, etc. It is not only necessary to live, but to make a living as well. The majority of students come to college with the realization that the college course, once completed, will assist them in some way or other to secure profitable employment. A college course successfully completed according to certain minimum standards is simply a requirement that must be fulfilled. For some this is the end of the matter, and they set out to meet the requirements. If they could secure the employment which they have in mind, with one or two years of college instead of four, they would willingly accept the curtailment and go to work. Their attitude toward education is businesslike.

2. *Necessity.* By this I mean the demands that are brought to bear on the student within the framework of the regular college discipline. Once you enter college, you have broken the ice and begun a new career. The new regime makes certain periodic demands which you must fulfill if you desire to continue in that regime. There are, for example, examinations, tests, written assignments, experiments, required reading, recitations, term papers, participation in debates, public speaking, etc. These demands are made peremptorily and with methodical regularity. They may not be to your liking. But they are immediate, pressing necessities created within the sphere of the career which you have chosen, and there is nothing to do but fulfill them as they occur or abandon that career.

3. *Personal distinction.* This is meant to include the desire to win honors or recognition among your own college group. Once you enter college you become a member of a new social group with its own standards of judgment. It has its heroes, champions and bigwigs, as well as their counterparts. You like to be a personage of importance, to be pointed out as a person of distinction. The desire to be thought of as good at something may actually help one to be good at something. This is not a motive for all students. It touches some with peculiar force, others but lightly and others imperceptibly or not at all. Whatever be the danger, worth or weakness of such a motive, it deserves a place in this enumeration.

4. *General desire to make good.* Going to college means that you have severed certain associations and connections and that you are now adrift upon a new career. It is a new undertaking, assumed after much serious deliberation and perhaps at a great expense. Having a valuable stake in the venture, it is natural that you should desire to make good. A certain amount of successful studying is the only thing that can make this venture a success.

5. *A sense of duty.* This is an upright attitude of moral responsibility in regard to studying. It is the opposite of that attitude which regards the daily tasks of life merely as so many chores which are to be evaded as adroitly or dispatched as quickly as possible. It is putting conscience in your work. The task of studying, then, is not merely a chore or a matter of option or an occupation which pays certain dividends, but a moral duty to be faithfully discharged. A student whom religion has trained to regard and perform the tasks of life as sacred duties of conscience is sustained in his studying by a purpose of singular force and significance.

6. *The satisfaction of intellectual interest.* This is an intellectual disposition that finds pleasure in the exercise of the mind and a satisfaction in the possession of truth. With such a disposition the student finds studying to be a pleasurable performance filled with subtle surprises and quiet exultations. Progress in understanding and knowledge often brings a peculiar joy and satisfaction which serve as active incentives to the labor of study and also as its satisfactory reward. Such a student is like a hunter who not only enjoys the results of the chase but the chase itself. The satisfaction of intellectual interest can be a genuine incentive to study. If this sounds a little unreal to you, answer these questions: Have you ever sat down to study because you liked it? Have you ever neglected one branch of study to spend more time studying another in order to satisfy a certain curiosity? Have you ever studied a subject to a point quite beyond class requirements? Then you have already had at least some experience with the motive which is here enumerated. We shall return to it later.

UTILITY

These are the purposes which singly or jointly underlie the effort of study. Usually the motive of utility takes the lead. In fact, most students come to college for the purpose of fitting themselves for some practical employment or profession. The whole college course with its entire curriculum of studies has a value in the student's mind because of its practical utility. But once his course is well on its way he finds himself immersed in quite a variety of studies. These are history, logic, French, mathematics and chemistry, for instance. His initial enthusiasm begins to wear down. The reason is because he cannot see clearly or appreciate keenly the utility of *each* of these branches. He must study one subject at a time, and there will surely be some branches whose ultimate value is not apparent. Utility, in order to function as an incentive, must narrow down and touch the matter that is being studied here and now. The broad, general appreciation that a college education is useful will not help you much to study French. French itself must be regarded as something of practical value. And here is your difficulty. The utility of French may now seem quite slight. Its utility is not obvious, but its difficulties are. At any rate the time when it will be useful seems remote and uncertain. A utility motive is only fully alive and active when the value of the thing studied stands out obvious, certain and immediate. A young man attending business college for three months has little difficulty getting up sufficient determination to put in long hours of study and practice at shorthand and typing. In his own mind the connection between these skills and getting employment is clearly grasped. The prospects of using them profitably is more or less certain, perhaps almost guaranteed, and the day when he can turn them to his advantage is "just around the corner." Little wonder, then, that the utility motive in his case operates with such effectiveness.

But the usefulness of the single branches of your curriculum—French, history, chemistry, etc.—have a different status. Their useful character is rather vaguely grasped. The chances of actually employing them to your advantage are more or less uncertain. At least the time when you can so employ them seems quite distant. Consequently, no matter how thoroughly you are convinced of the value and desirability of getting a college education, this broad purpose of general utility, when applied to this, that, and the other subject as they turn up in the curriculum, declines and almost vanishes as a motivating factor of study. Thus it happens that a student, although sincere in his general aspiration and vaguely realizing that he ought to study, wanders from subject to subject smitten and disastrously handicapped by a sense of grand inutility.

Still he may be an industrious student. When strong utility motives fail to mature, he may fall back on others more or less extrinsic, viz., his fear of failing, his general desire to make good, his ambition to win distinction and class honors, etc. What studying he does is principally a response to necessity, ambition or duty. These are indeed valuable incentives—they are the only ones some students have—but they are inferior, especially when they are the sole or dominant purpose of studying. Studying becomes a series of joyless, inefficient, sporadic efforts which may finally let the student down with a remorseful sense of little or nothing accomplished.

I do not mean to disparage the value or the propriety of the utility factor as a motive of studying. I have merely endeavored to point out that such a motive in respect to the individual subjects of the curriculum usually glimmers and functions with disappointing results. There should be a value, pragmatic or cultural, to every subject in the college curriculum. Moreover, I believe that, as a rule, there is such a value. The problem is that you should understand this value so that it becomes a purpose of sufficient force to induce you to study. Your difficulty is that you cannot so grasp this value at least in regard to each subject of the curriculum. For every student there are a certain number of subjects —logic, Latin, and mathematics are good examples—which he honestly regards as perfectly useless or quite unrelated to his ultimate life objectives. And no amount of explanation can succeed in making him understand that they might be of value to him. Or he may even be convinced that the matter is worthwhile learning but remains little moved by this conviction because the day when he envisions its actual use seems so distant.

IMPROVING THE UTILITY MOTIVE

This difficulty is not necessarily due to perversity, or to a lack of intelligence or to any want of serious purpose. It is a difficulty which is to be expected in any college student who has the energy which comes with youth, but not the perspective which comes from experience. No legerdemain of words can entirely remove the difficulty. But its magnitude can be reduced. In fact, I believe that it can be reduced to a point where you are able to appreciate the utility of the single branches of the course, including Latin, logic and mathematics, so that you will want to study them *because* they are useful. It is only at this point that utility becomes a motive of study. All this will be accomplished by modifying your attitude and considering the whole matter of your college curriculum from a new point of view.

Recall and reread what was said in the first chapter about the value of any subject taught in college. Each one has its usefulness. No branch of knowledge is useless. Naturally this is not apparent to you now. You lack the general background and the practical experience necessary to make such a judgment. This lack is not culpable; it is merely a fact to be admitted. But you can easily appreciate how your judgments change as experience grows. At one time in your career you were put through the rigors of grammar, spelling and simple arithmetic. Can you recall what your attitude toward these subjects was *then?* Did you ever try to get out of an arithmetic lesson? But how your estimation of these subjects has changed! How useful a knowledge of spelling and grammar is for writing a simple letter! How many problems of chemistry and physics have you solved with your knowledge of simple arithmetic? What a difference between then and now! Had anyone then attempted to make you realize the value of these simple subjects which you recognize now, the attempt would have been entirely futile. Thus our practical judgments in many things must wait for time and experience to correct and perfect.

In a similar way further experience and maturity will modify many of your practical judgments concerning the individual subjects of your college curriculum. If you are beginning the study of logic, for instance, you are not in the most favorable position to judge clearly its practical advantages. But once you have had some experience at analyzing carefully another's philosophy, at presenting arguments of your own, at planning an address or writing a book, the fundamentals of logic will seem to be most important equipment. In order to know the advantages of logic, you must first know logic and then have had experience in the actual application of it. Again, how little the Latin student can realize now that the Latin vocabularies which he learns with so much effort today will help him to command the terminology of science and philosophy! Nor can the novice in mathematics fully estimate how this subject, which annoys him with its abstractness, may be the master key to the understanding of a half a dozen or more sciences. Neither does a child catch the importance of correct posture till many years after he has learned it. Thus with experience comes a certain intellectual unfolding, and time ripens judgment. Your present verdicts of praise or condemnation of this or that study will not be the verdicts which you will pronounce ten years from today.

Moreover, as your education continues, it will gradually dawn upon you that certain branches of human knowledge are actually linked and correlated as units of one whole. Today the various branches of the curriculum may seem to stand out as so many pieces of knowledge isolated from and independent of one another. But this is not so. There are relationships between them. One dovetails with another and completes its understanding: mathematics with logic, philosophy with history, history with psychology, ethics with sociology, economics with religion, etc. The whole range of human knowledge, while it must be learned piece by piece, is not an aggregate of loose pieces, but of related pieces that fit into a more or less complete pattern. The separate branches of knowledge, like the pieces of a jigsaw puzzle, are best understood when viewed in relationship to the completed whole. If you are alert, this relatedness of various branches of knowledge may manifest itself with some clarity long before your college course is finished. The appreciation of this relatedness will mature with maturing vision. Intellectual horizons are never fixed. At any rate, the value of some subjects may now be understood dimly and with difficulty because you view them falsely, i.e., out of relationship to everything else.

Another factor which dulls your appreciation of the value of your individual studies is the apparent remoteness of the day when their value will become an actual advantage to you. Graduation Day seems quite a distant date. Your life objectives are set in the distant future. The day when you are forty years of age, independent and deep in the responsibilities of your chosen career, is such a long way removed from the present. Distant objectives seldom awaken enthusiasm and determination. But this remoteness of one's life work is one of the illusions of youth. It is difficult, though not impossible, for youth to appreciate the swift flight of time. Consider how quickly your high school days have fled. College days will pass as quickly. Your childhood days are already gone, but today you are nearly as close to those days of the past as you are to the important years of middle life. As you grow older years seem to shorten and time to pass more swiftly. Actually your life objectives, to which your college studies are related, are more immediate and proximate than you probably realize. Once you realize how near you actually are to the serious responsibilities of life, the value of each passing day and the significance of your studies stand out in such a clear, startling light that a strong incentive to study emerges almost immediately. One who is deeply impressed with the value of time is mentally conditioned for serious concentration.

INTELLECTUAL INTEREST

No one disputes that a clear conception of the utility of studying nourishes the incentive to study. I believe that such a purpose is the only incentive to which some people can respond. However, I am not sure that utility is the best ground for supporting a strong, permanent incentive. The most effective and lasting purpose is a simple, unaffected interest in the matter studied. It is possible to throw an almost unlimited amount of studious endeavor upon a given subject merely to satisfy an intellectual interest or curiosity. Utility purposes wane. Interest purposes tend to grow steadily; they carry the student much further and season the labor of study with a zest bordering on love.

Sometimes deep intellectual interests rise to dominate one's life without much deliberate forethought or conscious cultivation. They may be present before we are distinctly aware of them. They have come into control so gradually that we are unable now to trace their history or to account for their origin. This is an agreeable and fortunate experience, especially if it comes early in life, and there is nothing to do but to give these interests a clear track to forge full ahead.

"But can such an interest in study be developed?" I believe that it can, although I candidly admit that I believe that it is beyond the reach of some. There are some who are so constituted mentally that they learn little or nothing unless bluntly driven to it by vanity or immediate necessity. Vanity, entertainment and utility circumscribe their mental horizons. Yet vital intellectual interests are quite within the reach of many who do not actually possess them. One of the failures of modern education is that so many students pass through high school and college with no springs of enthusiasm touched, with no intellectual interests aroused, and destined to remain intellectually inarticulate.

But the case is not hopeless. The development of a deep interest in study can be developed even by mediocre students. One thing is certain: interest begins with knowledge. Knowledge begets interest and interest once begotten stimulates the desire to acquire more knowledge. The one reacts upon the other, but the starting point is knowledge. One cannot be interested in a subject without some konwledge of it, however little this knowledge is and however it is first acquired.

Since the starting point of interest in any subject is knowledge, you must begin by destroying your ignorance. Begin to know something about it, something certain and definite. Make the beginning with resolution and determination. This initial process of breaking the ice must simply be carried on bravely to the point where interest awakens. From there on the awakened interest begins to relieve the occupation of study of its laborious character. It tends to grow and may soon be strong enough to constitute such a strong motive that study becomes a pleasurable employment. You may then study the matter not to awaken an interest, but because you are already interested. When this point is reached, your concentration problem is considerably reduced, if not eliminated altogether.

Are you inclined to regard this as theoretical? Do you distrust your own native ability to acquire strong intellectual interests? You may have lived so long without such interests that you are inclined to doubt their existence or their practical character. But it is possible to destroy this skepticism and distrust by making a simple experiment. During vacation make a strong effort to acquire a definite knowledge in some field which is more or less unfamiliar to you, for instance, in geology, astronomy or radio. But the effort must be a serious one. Stick to a program of one hour of study each day for two weeks. Then note what happens. If you are of average intelligence and the work undertaken is not too far above your present level of education, you will probably experience the birth of a new interest in a matter which you had previously regarded as an alien subject. The interest may remain with you through life. In fact, many of the world's professional scholars and outstanding authorities in scientific fields—Joseph Priestly, chemist; William Herschel, astronomer; Gregor Mendel, botanist; Henri Fabre, entomologist—trod their way to fame by beginning in their respective fields as innocent and unsuspecting amateurs.

You never actually arouse all the intellectual interests of which you are capable, but many scholars have aroused so many and diverse interests that they begin to crowd upon one another and overtax the limited amount of time that anyone can give to study. Then arises the further problem of selecting which one should be allowed to predominate and which ones are to be set aside. But the problem of conflicting intellectual interests belongs to the mature scholar and need not be treated further in this book.

Suggestions

1. State in your own way the difference between a wish and a purpose. Illustrate each by a practical example drawn from your own experience.
2. Impartially examine and enumerate the motives which brought you to college. Which one is dominant? Would you study if there were no examinations? Would you quit college now if you could get a paying job?
3. Have you ever pursued a branch far beyond the regular demands of class work? Have you ever studied a subject which is not required? Have you ever studied during vacation? From your answers to these questions draw your own conclusions.
4. Do you know anyone who has mastered a subject without having gone to college or without the benefit of regular instruction? What was the motive? What does this indicate?
5. Do you think that college training as you know it is tending to develop any permanent intellectual or cultural interests? Do you think that college training should develop such interests? Are there any factors about your college which hinders or defeats the development of such interests?
6. Does graduation seem a long way off? Does this tend to retard your interest or efficiency?
7. Have you ever experienced a keen appreciation of the value of time? Can you attribute this to any particular fact or circumstance? Has such an appreciation acted as a real incentive to study?

CHAPTER VI

Rapid Reading

Mere reading is not to be identified with studying, but ordinarily studying does involve a great deal of reading. The amount of reading demanded of a student will vary widely with the subjects taken. A course in English necessitates considerably more reading than a course in chemistry. Sociology and history create a reading demand much greater than mathematics. But at any time in your career as a student the amount of reading to be done is one of considerable volume. Your ability to read rapidly and well will be an important factor of your success. The aim of this chapter is to assist you to acquire the skill of rapid reading.

HANDICAPS OF SLOW READING

Most students read too slowly. If you are an unusually slow reader, you labor under a definite handicap. Slow reading means a serious loss of time. In many cases it even hinders a good understanding of the matter read. When the eyes dawdle along the pages of a book with too frequent and too long pauses between the phrases and sentences read, the mind is invited to stray off to irrelevant interests. The penalty is a corresponding loss of understanding. Rapid reading is an important skill. It will save time, improve comprehension and make your studying more interesting.

MECHANICS OF READING

The first step in acquiring this skill is the understanding of the mechanics of reading. When you read, the eyes do not sweep across the printed line with a smooth, uniform rate of speed like a revolving camera. On the contrary, they leap across the page by a series of jumps, and between each jump there is a measurable pause. The number of pauses made in reading a single line of print varies with different readers; some make as few as three or four, others as many as ten. The number of words which the eye takes in a single jump in called the "perceptual span." The period of pause is called the "fixation." These fixation pauses also differ in length for different readers. The wider the span, the fewer fixations are required. While the eye pauses, the mind comprehends the meaning of the word or phrase just read. This is important. *Comprehension takes place at the fixation points.*

A single span may cover a single word, or it may cover a whole phrase or group of words. The following line may be read by some readers in four spans. "A lazy student wastes his time and ends his course with little achieved." Good reading does not require individual attention to each word. The phrase "a lazy student" can be caught by a single glance of the eye. The eye can be taught to recognize at once a whole phrase made up of several words, just as it recognizes at once a whole word made up of several letters. For example, when the words "philosophy" or "accomplishment" appear on the printed page, the eye does not attend to each single letter making up the word. The same words would be recognized just as quickly even if some of the letters were missing. If I were to write "philphy" you would still recognize the word. In a long word, the omission of a letter or two may not even be noticed. It is the length and general features of the printed word which render it instantly recognizable. To a certain degree the same principle holds good for the recognition of phrases or groups of words. In most cases, articles such as "the" and "a" and prepositions such as "on" or "at," etc., are slurred over or gathered in by a single glance of the eye together with the words they modify. The number of words which can be caught by the eye at a single glance may vary from one to six. Naturally the greater the number of words thus grouped toegther, the larger the span, and this means fewer fixations to a given line of print.

While the eye moves across a printed line by forward jumps and little pauses, there are also occasional movements of the eye backward over the word or phrase just read. You often catch yourself retracing a line of print just read. The movement of the eye backward over a part just read is called a "regression."

FACTORS OF SLOW READING

If you are a slow reader you will recognize some of the following factors in your own reading:

1. The slow reader plucks each word out of the printed line one by one. Each word receives equal attention.

2. There are rather long pauses between words and phrases and especially between sentences.

3. New and strange words appear now and then and halt the progress of reading till the words have had time to register in the mind.

4. There are numerous regressions. Phrases and sometimes entire sentences are retraced to clarify their meaning or to recover the trend of the thought.

5. There is unnecessary vocalization or articulation. Some readers actually whisper the words as they read or move the lips and tongue in an attempt to articulate the words. This, of course, chains down your rate of reading to the rate of your articulation. The eye can sweep a line of printed words three or four times faster than the tongue and lips can pronounce them.

6. If there is no actual vocalization, there is often a kind of suppressed articulation—slight movements of the tongue and a tension of the vocal cords.

7. Or there may be an unconscious attempt to imagine how the words would sound if they were pronounced. Some readers mentally sound the words as they read them. Reading becomes a kind of silent speech.

CAUSES OF SLOW READING

These habits of slow reading originate from several causes. Some of them are merely habits which you have carried over from your early school days when you were first taught the skill of reading. You perhaps learned to read by laboriously pronouncing each word aloud. When you were no longer required to read your lessons aloud, you never thoroughly discontinued the habit but substituted whispering or lip movements or some form of suppressed vocalization. And now for years you have gone along hampered by slow reading technique, acquired in the early stage of reading.

Slow reading may also be induced by the habitual reading of heavy material. This is particularly true of the serious student who has confined most of his reading to textbooks, encyclopedias and other forms of serious reading. Some books are written in more or less condensed style requiring slower reading than lighter material, such as news accounts and novels. Moreover, in your earnestness as a student, you have read such books with deliberate caution, marking what is important and pausing frequently in order to comprehend and remember. You have thus taught yourself slow reading, and the habit once acquired is now employed for all types of reading, regardless of the matter and content.

Another cause of slow reading is an insufficient vocabulary. New words met in reading command additional attention. You pause over them to get their meaning from the context and to look at their spelling. Anyone plunging into an unfamiliar and technical field of reading will notice at once how his reading progress is halted and interrupted at the occurrence of each new term. Ideally, then, a term should be so familiar that the mind recognizes it immediately and comprehends its meaning the instant the eye meets the sight of its printed form.

At times, other causes operate to retard your reading rate, such as poor health, excessive fatigue, poor vision or eye strain, lack of interest and worry. Such physical and mental conditions make attention difficult, the thread of the thought is lost and frequent regressions are needed to recapture it.

IMPROVING YOUR READING RATE

This analysis of slow reading is sufficient to suggest the remedies:

1. The first step toward rapid reading is to acquire the skill of "phrase reading." Stop plucking away at the individual words. Group the words into phrases. Take them in bundles. A phrase is a unit of thought and, provided the words are familiar, can be comprehended well by a single glance of the eye. A good reader cuts the matter up into chunks, and the eye advances along the printed line phrase by phrase in a kind of a rhythmic, regular flow allowing brief, necessary pauses between the phrases. The number of words which are thus gathered into a single phrase will differ according to the skill of the individual reader and the nature of the material which is being read.

Your "perceptual span" can be increased very easily to the point when it includes at least three or four words. A reading span of this length is necessary for ordinary effective reading. For a very slow reader, whose reading span is about one word, this would mean a considerable increase. The larger the span, the fewer fixations which are required to a line. Think of the great saving of time accomplished if you could reduce the number of fixations per line from eight to four. If the reading span averages about one word, and there is a fixation after each word, not only is there a loss of time, but also a serious hindrance to good understanding.

2. Accustom yourself to briefer fixations. This is a matter of extreme importance—of more importance than lengthening the span—because "approximately ninety-four percent of the time spent in reading a line is taken up by the pauses or fixations."* These pauses between the phrases

------

*Charles Bird, *Effective Study Habits* (New York: D. Appleton-Century Co.), p. 102.

read are really the comprehension period, i.e., during these pauses the mind grasps the meaning of the phrases. When the average time consumed by the fixations is reduced, there is a considerable gain in the reading rate.

Unnecessarily long pauses are often merely a bad reading habit which you have not learned to discard. In all ordinary reading of light matter their length can be notably reduced without injury to comprehension. There is, of course, no standard length for such pauses. Their length will depend upon the difficulty of the matter read or the reader's power to understand what he has read. A slow thinker must pause longer for comprehension than a fast thinker. Your native individual capacity for quick thinking will in many cases set the limit to your reading rate.

3. Reduce the number of regressions to a minimum. Frequent regressions may also be a matter of habit, in which case the defect can be easily eliminated by a little determination and practice. But in all reading there are occasional unavoidable regressions due to unfamiliar technical words, new idioms, loss of interest, etc. A good reader does not regress unnecessarily, but only to capture some subtlety or difficult thought which his mind did not clearly grasp at first.

4. Learn the technique of silent reading. Don't whisper the words to yourself. Don't even attempt to vocalize the words at all. The lips, tongue and vocal cords should be entirely at ease. Reading, then, is merely the mechanical action of the eye covering the printed characters, with attention to their meaning but with no throat effort to produce sound. Don't even try to imagine how the words would sound if they were spoken. Pass directly from the sight of the word to the comprehension of its meaning. Some investigators seem to doubt if articulatory efforts can be completely eliminated, but effective rapid reading at least requires their reduction to the lowest possible minimum.

It should be clearly understood that the elimination of vocalization is treated here only as far as it contributes to rapid reading. I do not advise rapid reading and, hence, do not advise the elimination of vocalization for all types of reading material. There are times when it is wise and useful to vocalize and to read slowly, to think how the words would sound if spoken or read aloud, even times to read aloud to oneself. Poetry, orations and beautiful passages of picturesque prose conceal much of their beauty and charm in the sound of the words. There are felicitous expressions, beautiful lines and whole passages of sublime prose which must be fairly spoken as they are read, if we are to derive maximum profit and pleasure in reading them. For there is a certain beauty and majesty in the very sound and rhythm of words. Besides, there are passages containing thoughts which in themselves have such tenderness, beauty and depth that they deserve to be read slowly and thoughtfully. Vocalization, including reading aloud to oneself, may also be necessary in preparing a passage which we are to declaim or read before an audience, in order to train the ear for sound effects. The same type of reading sometimes assists the reader in analyzing, for instance, a difficult section of philosophy where the thought follows a strictly logical sequence, and much depends upon the proper emphasis of a single word or upon due attention to qualifying phrases likely to be slurred over by silent reading. A rapid reader must have his hand on the throttle and be prepared at all times to slow down, even to come to a full stop, and to speed ahead, just as the content of the material read or purpose of the reading decrees. It would be stupid to race through a beautiful poem, where so much depends upon rhythm and sound effects, at the same rate as you would read the morning paper. Notwithstanding, rapid reading is a technique most important for the student since most of the material which he reads is read merely for the sake of grasping its meaning.

5. Establish a copious vocabulary, both general and technical. The establishment of an extensive knowledge of words cannot, of course, be done at once, and it is a work that is never fully completed. A fuller treatment of this subject follows in a subsequent chapter.

6. Physical and mental health may affect reading, as well as your general scholastic success. This factor, because of its unique importance, will also be left for a separate and subsequent treatment.

SETTING RULES TO PRACTICE

You now know the mechanics of reading and the principal steps which are necessary to increase your reading rate. But this knowledge alone will not suffice. What you now need is the determination to put this knowledge to use. Consistent, deliberate practice at rapid reading will almost always bring surprising results.

Set aside one period a day for this practice. These periods need not be lengthy. Ten or fifteen minutes daily will suffice. Do your practicing on light material—novels, simple narration, news accounts or any kind of reading matter of a simple nature and does not strain your general knowledge of words.

You will find experimenting with yourself a profitable and interesting process. Take a simple novel and read the first half at your ordinary slow rate. Make an accurate record of the time spent at reading; compute the number of words which are read in a given time and then determine the number of words per minute. Then read the second half of the novel at top speed, putting into practice all the suggestions given above. Going at top speed, many phrases and sentences will be lost, but do not regress. Your aim now is merely to hold the thread of narration. As long as you are doing that forge forward with the maximum rapidity. Then check the number of words read per mintue and compare this record with the record for the first half. The difference between the two records will surprise you.

Try reading an entire novel at your maximum speed, omitting phrases, sentences and whole sections of descriptive matter which are not essential to the progress of the narration. If you start a lengthy passage which begins to describe how the bride was dressed on her wedding day, resolve to skip that section. By digging into the passage at isolated points you can easily see whether or not the description is continuing. You do not need to know whether a dress is white satin or pink silk to understand the narration. You can dress the bride up in your own imagination any way you please, and she will be charmingly clad, which in most cases will be quite sufficient. Not every sentence that an author writes needs to be read. Anyway, when the description is past, pick up the narration and continue it. You will be disturbed and a little shocked that you are going so fast, but never mind. Remember your purpose. You are not proofreading, nor reading to analyze, nor to criticize, nor to appreciate the style and choice of words. You are merely practicing silent reading for speed. When you have finished, compute the number of words read per minute and compare with your ordinary slow rate.

Keep practicing more rapid reading at all times, no matter when, where or what you read, and check your reading rate month by month. It will show a marked improvement in speed.

"How much can one improve his rate of reading?" This is difficult to say. Some authorities claim that a slow reader may easily accelerate his speed, without loss of comprehension, from fifty to a hundred percent. Think what a great advantage you would gain by establishing a permanent rate of reading just fifty percent greater than your present one.

STANDARD RATE

You may be prone to ask, at this point, "What is the standard rate?" There is no standard rate of good rapid reading. How rapidly one reads depends on too many varying conditions to be able to set down a definite all-round standard rate. The rate at which one reads will vary with the kind of material read. History can be read faster than philosophy. It also depends on the style of the author. For some authors put their thoughts down in such involved, complex sentence structures that even an experienced and rapid reader is slowed down to a trickle when he attempts to read them. Others write in a style so simple that sentences are turned into sense as quickly as the eye covers them. It also depends upon the purpose of the reader, whether it be to analyze, criticize or to amuse himself, and on the interest in the matter read, for when interest flows at full tide, there is better concentration and, hence, fewer distractions and regressions. It may also depend upon the condition of one's mental and physical health, vision, lighting conditions, etc.

Besides, no good reader works through a book or a long reading assignment with a uniform speed throughout. Some passages are read at his top speed, others at his middle speed and others may be taken in "low."

Some attempts have been made, however, to ascertain a fair rate of reading as to certain types of material. "A good adult should read a minimum of from 250 to 300 words a minute of textbook or nonfiction material of average difficulty."*

"For textbook reading of a straightaway nature we may fairly expect ourselves to average about 225 words per minute."†

My advice is don't annoy yourself by comparing your rate with any approximate standard rate. The principal thing is to determine your own rate of reading and then proceed to improve that. Improve yourself to the utmost of your ability and forget about standard rates.

DOES RAPID READING IMPAIR COMPREHENSION?

The insistence I have placed on the desirability of rapid reading may lead to the question, "Does rapid reading impair comprehension?" Reading may indeed be so rapid that comprehension is impaired. But that kind of rapid reading is nowhere advised in these pages. The goal should be *to read with the minimum consumption of time without loss of understanding of the matter read.* There is scarcely anyone who cannot greatly accelerate his rate of reading without the slightest injury to good comprehension.

Slow reading is not necessarily reading with good comprehension. Sometimes it is merely slovenly habit. Or it may be the effect of poor comprehension and slow thinking. Perhaps you read slowly because you comprehend poorly. Or, reversely, too slow reading may be a contributing cause of poor comprehension. Perhaps you do not comprehend well because you read too slowly. When you read by phrases with brief fixations and with fewer regressions, in other words rapidly, you may

---

*C. Gilbert Wrenn, and Luella Cole, *How to Read Rapidly and Well* (California: Stanford University Press), p. 11.

†Leal A. Headley, *How to Study in College* (New York: Henry Holt & Co.), p. 226.

find that comprehension of the material read has actually improved. But even if there is no improvement in the matter of comprehending, there are still the advantages of a great saving in time and added interest.

STRIKING YOUR STRIDE

Whatever your rate of reading may be in regard to a given kind of material, you do not strike your maximum efficiency at once. In beginning to read a book, for instance, there is a "warming-up" period. During this initial period you are getting acquainted with the names of the characters, the peculiarity of the author's style, etc. Gradually you hit your stride. But once the maximum rate is reached, other factors being the same, it can be sustained.

Once you have set out to improve the rate of your reading, there is usually an interval of awkwardness and inefficiency. For a while you may be reading even at a slower rate than customary. But do not be discouraged and never yield to the temptation of turning back to your old way of reading. This is merely a period of adjustment, and some inefficiency and clumsiness are to be expected in any attempt to reform an old habit and acquire a new skill.

Rapid reading is one of the easiest skills to learn and once established always bestows rich rewards upon its possessor.

Suggestions

1. Give the meaning of the following terms: perceptual span, fixation, regression, vocalization, phrase reading.
2. When is it advisable to read aloud?
3. Accurately test your own reading rate in ordinary, light material. Then practice rapid reading as suggested in this chapter for a period of ten days. Test your reading rate again and note the improvement.
4. Search the files of your library for books on the subject of reading. This is a subject which deserves investigation. You will find a great deal of help in any one of the following books: *Reading* by John A. O'Brien; *On the Art of Reading* by Sir A. T. Quiller-Couch; *Silent and Oral Reading* by Clarence R. Stone.

CHAPTER VII

Remembering

Learning is not identical to remembering, but learning would be useless without it. If you were to forget everything as quickly as you learned it, you would remain in permanent ignorance. Memory retains what you learn and holds it ready for use when you need it. Memory gives value to learning, and the two processes, although quite distinct, are related and inseparable.

LEARNING AND REMEMBERING

It is quite apparent that both the ability to learn and the ability to remember vary widely in different individuals. But it is not so generally recognized that your ability to learn does not necessarily determine your ability to remember. The two mental capacities, i.e., to learn and to remember, may be associated in four different ways. Roughly speaking, there are four types of minds:

1. "Those whose minds are as lead to learn; and as lead to remember.
2. "Those whose minds are as steel to learn; and as steel to remember.
3. "Those whose minds are as steel to learn; and as lead to remember.
4. "Those whose minds are as lead to learn; and as steel to remember."*

In the first group are students who learn quickly and almost as quickly forget. With them, nothing sticks although they have little difficulty understanding.

In the second group are students who learn with difficulty but remember well what they have once learned. Things "stick" after they are once acquired. It is generally supposed that "hard learners" are good at "retaining," but this is not universally true.

The third group of students learn with difficulty and quickly forget

---

*Headley, *How to Study in College*, pp. 132-33.

what they have learned. They are a very unfortunate group for their poor memory is constantly robbing them of the fruit of their hard mental labor.

The fourth group of students learn with the maximum ease and retain what they learn with minimum effort. Little is lost through the meshes of memory. Lord Macaulay and Saint Thomas Aquinas belonged to this fortunate group.

CAN MEMORY BE IMPROVED?

Whoever you are, you belong, at least approximately, to one of these four groups. Whatever may be your ability to learn, God has also given you a certain ability to retain or remember. Such expressions as "I have no memory" are not, of course, literally true. Every normal person remembers past experiences and past learning to a certain degree. The normal life of an individual could not proceed for a single day unless he retained in memory a considerable portion of his past experiences. Whatever may be the degree of your native ability to remember, it is probably a fixed quantity and cannot be improved much throughout your lifetime. If your memory is like lead, it will never become like steel.

But this need not discourage you. There remains before you a wide field of improvement not in your fundamental, natural ability to remember, but in the *method of remembering*. By using the proper methods, the efficiency of your memory can be remarkably improved. This may seem like a contradiction. But it is a truth which should encourage anyone who is distressed by the handicap of a poor memory. Give a child a fulcrum and a lever, and he can lift as much as a giant with his raw, muscular strength. Thus the inferior strength of a child, if supplemented by the right kind of instruments, may be a match for superior naked power. Proper "memory methods" are like the fulcrum and the lever. They do not enhance, at least to any marked degree, the original power of remembering, but they can improve the performance of memory. Your natural power of remembering may be considered as more or less fixed. It is not like a muscle which can be extraordinarily strengthened by exercise. But by employing the proper methods, your memory may reach achievements which you now consider quite beyond its range.

So take your general power to remember as it is and learn how to use it. Many people complaining of poor memories could do wonderfully well if they went about the business of remembering with the proper technique. To improve the method or technique of remembering, the following suggestions are offered. Study them well and practice them consistently. Your better memory performance may surprise you.

GENERAL SUGGESTIONS

1. *Don't try to remember everything.* Learn to discriminate between what is worth remembering and what is not. To a certain degree you practice this principle every day. No sensible person tries to remember every news item he reads in the morning newspaper. Many things we hear and read are quite trivial, which, even if they were remembered successfully, would merely load the mind without enriching it. The gist of things is often quite sufficient. A general idea unencumbered with minute details and specifications is often quite satisfactory for practical purposes. What value is there in remembering every single character in a novel? Remembering four or five of the principal characters should be sufficient. We might quite profitably remember the king's name and as profitably forget the name of the king's butler. Many items in a lecture or a textbook lesson are purely introductory in nature, or merely serve to lead the mind to the understanding of a certain point or to illustrate and clarify it. When you get the point, the rest may often be disregarded.

Moreover, a successful effort to remember a few things is a million times more valuable than an attempt to remember a dozen things, which fails completely. Several years ago while traveling in the Rocky Mountains with a guide, I endeavored to remember the names of the strange trees that were pointed out to me. But their number grew so large that I soon discovered that my memory was tortured and overtaxed with the effort to remember them all. So I resolved to retain the names of only four of the more common trees and not to bother about the rest. I did succeed easily in remembering the names of four, which was at least a comfortable acquisition. Had I tried to remember all of them, I would probably have forgotten them all. In studying an assignment or reading a book do not torture yourself trying to remember everything. It is an impossible task anyway. Select the outstanding items and try to remember only these. To try to remember everything is to meet discouragement. Select with care the things you want to remember and complacently resign yourself to forget the rest. This, of course, requires decision and discrimination between what is important and what is not. But the very mental effort to decide and to discriminate will help you to remember.

Then there are other items of knowledge which, although quite important, need not be committed to the care of the memory, v.g., miscellaneous and statistical information, because they can always be found when needed. Encyclopedias, reference books, atlases, etc., carry large stocks of information which can be turned to your use with a few moments of search and consultation. It may be of use for me at sometime to know the eighty-eight counties of Ohio and their county seats, but it would be quite imprudent to attempt to memorize them as I once did. I may at sometime, indeed, require such detailed knowledge, but when I do I can quickly turn to my atlas, which will furnish me all the needed information within a few minutes. It may be useful to me at sometime to know the suicide rate for the various states in the country. But I know exactly where to turn to get this information and this is quite sufficient. Addresses and telephone numbers, etc., are needed from day to day, but don't try to burden your memory with them. Write them down in a handy book or on a card, and then the needed information will be at your disposal whenever you require it.

Don't aspire, then, to be an animated encyclopedia. But remember where to find things when you need them. This is a mark of a truly efficient, educated man.

2. *Get a good original impression of what is to be remembered.* When a thing comes into the mind clearly and vividly, its future retention is relatively easy. An obscure, hazy impression sentences the matter almost certainly to quick oblivion. We fail to remember many things simply because they were never clearly and vividly established in the mind. One distinct impression is better than a dozen faint ones. Here is a familiar experience: You are introduced to a person, have heard his name pronounced several times and have spent an hour conversing with him. The next day you are unable to recall his name, to say definitely whether he wore glasses or not or to tell whether his suit was brown or gray. Have you a poor memory? Perhaps you have a very fine memory but failed to remember these particular items merely because they were never firmly fixed in your mind by a clear, vivid impression. Everyone has had the experience of passing a certain house a hundred times without being able to remember anything definite about it, walking down a street and noticing its name a hundred times without being able to recall it, etc. Mere mechanical, casual repetitions serve the memory poorly. But if a thing is once stamped into the mind sharply and clearly, the mind will retain it with comparative ease. Don't complain of your bad memory if you have not given it a fair chance.

There are several ways to make our original impression of things clear and vivid.

a. *The first is to intend to remember.* Some students read over an assignment casually and trust to luck that it will "stick." If your assignment is the War of the Roses, study it with the definite intention to remember and to remember certain important things: What caused it? Who fought it? When was it fought? How long did it last? The man who sets out on a vacation with the intention of remembering the interesting and unusual experiences in order to record them in a diary will return with a better memory of these experiences than one who moves along and just allows experiences to happen. When you read an English assignment for the purpose of making a report of it, your memory of the characters and plot is far superior to its usual performance because you read it with an intention to remember. The intention always serves to make the mental reception sharp and clear.

b. *Impressions are clarified by interest and attention.* These two factors, interest and attention, are always closely related in the work of study. Interest in a subject rivets attention, and the two together offer valuable assistance to good remembering. Examples abound in everyone's experience to illustrate how a lack of interest diminishes the ability of the mind to retain. A garden lover may show you his flowers and tell you distinctly the names of them, but unless you are interested in flowers, their names will seldom be retained. One may listen politely to a conversation without being able to recall much of its substance because he had no interest in it. But if you are introduced to a friend and you become interested in him, remembering his name and the things he said is quite easy. A student has little difficulty remembering lessons in subjects which have aroused a keen interest. But he often complains of a poor memory when he attempts to remember material which has never deeply interested him. Whatever a student can do to invest his subject with a lively interest will serve to vivify his impressions of it and make the remembering of it more certain and much easier.

c. *Sometimes artificial devices can be employed to create a clear-cut impression.* If you have special difficulty remembering a name or a date, write it across a piece of paper in large, bold letters. Look at its several syllables. Repeat it aloud. Pronounce it clearly, forcibly, even with a vengeance. If you can make the process thrilling or laughable, so much the better. Never mind if this seems like a foolish procedure. Only keep in mind its purpose, namely to secure a clear, deep impression of the thing learned. Memory will then do its work of retaining with gratifying efficiency. This suggestion, however, is of limited application.

3. *Understand what is to be remembered.* It is folly and a waste of time to attempt to memorize a passage before understanding its meaning. Of what lasting good is it to hand over to memory a piece of material which you don't understand? Putting memory before understanding is a perversion. With such a perverted process, the work of remembering can only be accomplished by monotonous drill and countless repetitions, all demanding an extra toll in time and labor. And even if the matter is finally established in the memory by such costly effort, the process of forgetting sets to work immediately and soon reduces it to complete oblivion. The effort to remember is thus raised to the maximum with the very minimum of results.

Students with good retentive powers often are tempted to substitute memorizing for learning. Every geometry teacher has met them. A proposition in geometry is not learned by merely memoriing it. But if it is easier for you to memorize than to understand it, which may be true in certain cases, you are in danger of loading the mind at the expense of arresting the understanding. If studying ever becomes synonymous to you with memorizing, you are destined to be a very mediocre and unoriginal thinker.

If, then, you are to remember a lesson, a proposition in geometry or a history assignment, your first step is to understand it thoroughly. You never understand a matter thoroughly unless you can restate it in your own words. The words which an author uses are to convey his thoughts to you. They are not meant to serve as a model for you to express the same matter to others. Hence, in grappling with any difficult lesson, acquire the habit of using original illustrations and talking the matter over with yourself as if some interested person were listening. At any rate get the thing into your own mind. When that is done, the work of remembering is already largely accomplished.

Sometimes a passage like a quotation, a definition or a poem must be memorized verbatim. But even here the principle holds good. First review the entire passage, searching out its meaning. Then note its general form and sentence structure. The tedium of memorizing will then be reduced to the minimum.

But under no circumstances crowd the memory with material which has not been mentally digested. If you want to remember something of length or complexity, first understand it.

4. *Establish material in the mind in systematic, logical units whenever possible.* A series of unconnected words, like "jump," "cat," "rail," "squirrel," "big," "catch," "fence," are certainly much more difficult to remember than the same words when knitted into a meaningful sentence like "The cat jumped over the rail fence to catch the big squirrel." In the latter case the words form a logical whole. They are related units in a plan. Thus each word when fitted into a definite place helps you to recall any of the others. What can be done with *words* can be done with *facts. Tether your facts into bundles of connected thought.* To remember, for the rest of your life, that Marietta, Ohio, was founded in 1788 might seem to be rather difficult. But the effort to remember this fact is reduced to practically nothing if you relate it to the formation of the Northwest Territory in 1787. This latter date is one of the most important in American history and has been in your mind since childhood. But the formation of the Northwest Territory really led up to the founding of Marietta in 1788. The two facts are actually related in history as cause and effect. They should be logically related in your mind. It is practically as easy to remember two facts as one, if they are related

in a logical unit. For a historian, no date or event stands out in naked relief. It is always a significant link in a connected chain. Relate new facts to problems, to your individual experiences, to other facts already learned. Compare things; contrast things. Put them together somehow and tie them up in significant wholes. Once the connection is made and things are understood as a whole, the individual items composing it sit securely in the mind and are easily recalled when necessary. A librarian could never pick a given book from the stacks unless all the books were arranged in systematic groups. If the books were stood up in the shelves one after the other with no order or system, no single book could be found when it was wanted and for all practical purposes would be lost. Similarly, we often encounter men who have done an enormous amount of reading but who have little facility at remembering anything they have read. Unless a new fact taken into the mind is immediately associated with something else which is already there, that fact is like a misplaced book in a great library.

Of course, turning material learned into logical relationships requires considerable mental effort. But this merely illustrates a principle which, by this time, you have probably discovered for yourself: *good remembering is conditioned by the right kind of thinking.* Once the practice of binding things into logical units has become established, the mind can retain a vast amount of material with comparative accuracy and ease. There is also the consolation that "as we grow older, if the organization of our knowledge is improving, the power of reproducing it will likewise be increasing."*

But the above principle cannot be applied to everything which is to be remembered. It is useless to attempt to associate things into logical connections when the things themselves are not logically connected. There are many fragmentary items of knowledge which simply must be memorized by rote. This requires drill and repetition. Although there is an unintelligent prejudice against drilling for the learning of some things, there is no substitute for it. The student of a foreign language must simply admit the fact that most of the new foreign words must be learned by rote. If I am to remember the telephone number 7987, there is nothing to do but learn it that way. For I can find no logical connection, nor any other kind of connection, between the isolated numbers.

There are cases, however, where the mind may establish more or less artificial associations between isolated items to be remembered, giving valuable assistance to memory. The telephone number 3366 may be easily remembered by noting that the last two numbers are exactly dou-

---

*F. M. McMurry, *How to Study and Teaching How to Study* (Boston, New York & Chicago: Houghton Mifflin Co.), p. 171.

ble the first two. If you have difficulty with remembering the spelling of the adverb "there," tending to confuse it with "their," you can settle the matter by associating "there" with "here" and "where." If a student of botany learning the parts of a flower is prone to confuse "pistil" and "stamen," he can learn to clear his mind of all confusion by associating "pistil" with "pestle," whch is an instrument shaped like a billy club and very closely resembling the actual shape of the "pistil." If you are suddenly confronted with the necessity of remembering a series of things like "lemons," "eggs," "apples" and "nutmeg," you can take the first letter of each of these words and make them spell the single word "l-e-a-n." Remembering this single word will help you to remember the four given items with ease. Such artificial devices, especially like the latter one, are called *mnemonics*.

Some investigators discourage the use of mnemonics entirely. I see no reason for a universal condemnation of their use. If certain items, difficult to remember, cannot be put into some organized logical unit— and there are such—why not tie them up in any kind of artificial association which will assist the mind in retaining them? Some things are to be remembered for a short time to serve a special occasion, after which they may be profitably forgotten. In such cases, mnemonics may offer the most convenient, secure method of memory assistance. Besides, an artificial system may serve to establish some important matter well in mind after which the system, having served its purpose, may be discarded. Scaffolding is dismantled and discarded after the building has been completed. So the discreet use of mnemonics or any kind of artificial device may be efficiently employed on spare and special occasions to retain fragmentary material which cannot be fitted into a logical organization. After all, the business of the mind is to remember, and whatever aids the mind to remember helps.

5. *Several distributed efforts at memorizing are quite superior to one long, continuous period of concentrated effort.* If you are to memorize a poem or a speech, for instance, three distributed periods of study of twenty, ten and ten minutes respectively are more efficient than one long, concentrated study period lasting forty minutes. Some authors definitely say that the method of distributed effort is "from 25 to 50% more effective for purposes of permanent retention."*

The efficiency gained by spacing several periods of concentrated memory work, which has been experimentally proven, is easy to understand. To memorize efficiently requires complete attention and vigorous, sustained concentration. But this is hard mental work, which quickly

---

*Edward S. Jones, *Improvements of Study Habits* (New York: Henry Stewart Inc.), p. 38.

brings on fatigue, reduced interest, ennui and disgust. When these factors enter the study process, high efficiency is at once impaired. So do your verbatim memory work in relatively short periods, while the mind can bear down on the matter with its utmost concentration and maximum efficiency. But never continue the effort to the point of weariness or exhaustion. Memorizing periods may be interrupted by other studying, recreation or sleep. There is experimental evidence which points to the truth, long recognized by earnest students, that things committed to memory are better retained if the memorizing period is followed by sleep.

6. *The "whole method" is generaly more effective than the "part method."* This principle applies to all matter, whether it is to be remembered in gist form or verbatim.

The "whole method" takes a given piece of material and goes over it in its entirety a repeated number of times until the entire material is settled in the memory. In memorizing a speech, for instance, you thoughtfully read over the speech in its entire form, without giving any delayed or special attention to any individual paragraph or section. Then you read over the entire speech again and again. As the readings continue you will note that certain sentences and outstanding sections are gradually stamped in the memory with little effort. With each successive reading, the details and intervening matter, one after the other, fill in gradually and progressively until the whole speech finally becomes established in the memory. At the end of the process only a few of the more slippery and difficult passages will need individual attention and drill, but that is all.

The "part method" attacks the material to be remembered in piecemeal fashion, i.e., by memorizing one sentence or paragraph at a time, then another and another till the whole material is finally covered.

The "whole method" has the advantage of making the matter "stick" better when it is once learned because it comes into the mind from the beginning in its full logical pattern. During the whole process of memorizing, the mind has never considered the matter as anything but a logical unit. From the first to the last the full pattern of the speech is before the mind with all its logical links and climaxes. You get the "swing" and the "highlights" at once. Each successive reading serves to tighten this logical comprehensive grip. Things thus settled in the mind are retained much better than if they are laid in piece by piece like a mosaic of fragmentary bits.

If the matter thus memorized is intended for public delivery, perhaps as an oration or an address, this method has the added advantage—the delivery of the speech incurs fewer chances of being ruined by the memory slipping up on an isolated word or sentence. One who has learned a speech by this method does not hopelessly depend upon one sentence suggesting the next one. So if a sentence or two, even a whole paragraph, momentarily slips his memory, he does not come embarrassingly to a complete halt. With the framework of the speech in his mind, he is enabled either to extemporize without confusion till the needed thought arrives or else to pass over to the next link of thought without embarrassment or loss of time.

The "whole method" will not reveal its full merit to you unless you actually try it. At first it may seem to have the disadvantage of being a slow process. But this disadvantage is only apparent. It does *seem* slow because actual progress in memorizing is not experienced at once. At first, you do not seem to be memorizing at all. You may have read over the entire speech carefully without consciously committing more than two or three sentences to mind. If you are expecting quick results this may be discouraging. But the passages remembered accumulate rapidly with successive readings. It is actually the shorter method. Even if the "whole method" is not as speedy as the "part method," the confident, understanding grip and the security against little lapses of memory which this process assures would justify the additional time it may require.

If the material to be remembered is unusually long, it should be divided into several distinct parts, and the "whole method" may be employed on each separate part.

However, the "part method" may be more profitably employed by children and even by adults who are unable to grasp logical relationships. Ordinarily I would not advise its use on material of any great length and especially not on material which is to be addressed to an audience. One who memorizes a speech, for example, by attacking it line by line, paragraph by paragraph makes the remembering of each line dependent upon remembering the line previous. Herein lurks the danger that a single forgotten line may halt the process of memory entirely with embarrassing and disastrous results.

While I have explained the "whole method" in connection with *verbatim* memory, it may be usefully employed in all cases requiring remembering things in gist form. You may employ it to remember the content of a history assignment, a lesson in mathematics or a chapter in logic.

7. *Overlearning helps to clamp a thing securely in the mind.* By "overlearning" I mean studying over material several times *immediately* after it has been first learned. When you have finally learned your lesson in chemistry and feel satisfied that you understand it, you ordinarily lay the job aside and call it finished. But if you want to clinch the material definitely and decisively, proceed immediately to "overlearn" it, viz., to

study it over two or three times extra. The overlearning process may require an additional five or ten minutes. But these few extra minutes produce amazing results for good remembering.

If you really want to retain what you work so hard to learn, don't stop dead still just at the point when the matter is first learned. The reason for this is *the process of forgetting begins immediately after a thing has been learned.* No sooner has the mind understood than it begins to forget. You must acknowledge that you have a "forget-ory" as well as a memory. Your "forget-ory" starts to work immediately after the mind has made its original acquisition. Not only does the process of forgetting set in *immediately,* but the rate of forgetting is most rapid during the first few hours following the learning. The forgetting process works with tremendous and devastating speed during the first few hours after you have stored the mind with knowledge. Within eight hours after a lesson has been learned sixty percent of it may be already forgotten. After the first eight to ten hours the rate of forgetting slows down. This fact, that so much of our knowledge is scheduled for such speedy oblivion, should arouse any student to the need of salvaging the precious acquisition of long hours of laborious learning. Overlearning is one way to salvage the fruits of hard study. It may require a little determination and will power, but the few extra minutes that it requires are the most valuable employment of time that you can make. "To stop studying when a lesson can barely be recalled is like getting a fish on the hook and not bothering to land it."*

The rapidity of the forgetting process, when not checked by overlearning, suggests very clearly why the laborious and prodigious effort of cramming leaves the crammer with so little permanent knowledge. It also indicates why learned lectures, forums and public discussions are so disappointing from the standpoint of permanent, worthwhile intellectual results. Neither the laborious crammer nor the passive lecture fan is inclined to take time to expend the effort to overlearn.

8. *Remembering is aided by recall.* This process differs, but only in degree, from overlearning. Overlearning is the immediate reinforcement of what has just now been learned with the view of making it relatively permanent. Recall is studying the matter over later—a month, a year, or several years later—to keep the material intact. Headley compares the work of recall to thrifty repair work, which is made occasionally on a good building to prevent the process of deterioration (p. 152). No matter how soundly a thing has been learned and fixed in the mind, masses and whole chunks of material will crumble away with the passage of the months and years. If you are anxious to prevent this inevitable deteriora-

---

*Headley, *How to Study in College,* p. 151.

tion and to restore its losses, seasonable periods of recall, adjusted to your purpose and needs, are necessary.

Seriously restudying what has once been learned, besides reinforcing the memory in its regard, broadens and deepens your knowledge. No student can possibly understand at first all the hidden implications and significances of a given section of history or philosophy, for example, even when these matters have been thoroughly and solidly learned. As often as the matter is recalled—I mean earnestly restudied—new lights, new connections with other facts, new meanings and new problems will always reveal themselves. Once you have learned a thing well, no matter what it is, from that moment on, it is always in a process of an interesting, fascinating unfoldment. The enjoyment of these continuous disclosures, the unfolding, expanding significance of things is one of the richest rewards of a mature student.

UNLIMITED CAPACITY

You must get along for the rest of your life with whatever natural ability to remember God has given you. But whatever this natural ability may be, its efficiency of performance can be increased to a surprising degree by employing proper methods and technique. Having learned these, your future accomplishments of better remembering are largely a matter of determination and practice. With correct methods of studying and thinking, your mind should grow richer as you grow older.

You should be encouraged by the fact that there is absolutely no limit to the extent of material which a given memory can effectively retain. Your mind is not like a bucket which can be filled to the brim and then hold no more. One thing well learned and remembered immediately helps you to remember other things. Logical connections and relationships increase, new associations multiply, facts dovetail with facts and all the time the load grows without becoming heavier.

Suggestions

1. Can you explain how learning and remembering are distinct but related processes? Is it true that one who learns easily forgets easily? That one who learns with difficulty effectively retains what he learns?
2. Can you reconcile these two propositions:
    a. One's natural ability to remember does not improve with age or practice.
    b. One may improve his memory performance by using the proper methods.

3. Have you observed that your own memory has improved with age or with practice?
4. From your own experience give an example of forgetting a thing because it had never been clearly and firmly established in your mind. Did you complain of having a bad memory?
5. Discuss these propositions:
   a. Good remembering is conditioned by good thinking.
   b. A thing well learned is half-remembered.
6. Take a history lesson and set it up in the mind as a logical unit and experience for yourself how your memory is assisted thereby to retain it.
7. Do you use mnemonics? When should you not use them?
8. Why are several distributed efforts at memorizing more effective than one long, concentrated effort?
9. Be sure that you understand what is meant by the "whole method." Discuss its advantages.
10. Reread a book which you read five years ago. You will then be able to discuss on the basis of your own experience the advantages of "overlearning" and "recall."
11. Is a poor memory the same as absentmindedness? What ordinarily is the cause of absentmindedness?

CHAPTER VIII

Learning

Not all minds are alike in their natural ability to comprehend. But no matter what the quality of one's natural talents may be, the method of learning or the way you go about it may be either a hindrance or an aid. Excellent natural talents are sometimes hindered by an inefficient technique, while mediocre talents often achieve excellent results by merely employing an efficient technique. The present chapter will treat upon certain methods of studying which may aid you in your business of learning.

MASTERING AN ASSIGNMENT

We are concerned here with the student's attempt to master a given assignment or lesson of an informative nature. It may be a lesson in the textbook, a reading assignment in an encyclopedia, an essay, etc. Two ways of approach are in vogue among students unskilled in the technique of studying.

One student simply reads the lesson over more or less thoughtfully with some special attention to the more important points, possibly winding up with a quick review of some of the difficult parts. He thus satisfies himself that the matter has been learned and trusts that his memory will "deliver the goods" upon future demand. Such a student is often caught in examination by "surprise" questions demanding information which he is sure is not contained in the text. On returning to the text he is surprised again that the information demanded is really there. Or he may suddenly discover that his memory does not surrender the matter so completely nor so accurately as he had expected.

Another student, more conscientiously and methodically inclined, tries the "piecemeal" method. He learns the matter section by section. He labors over each section or passage as it occurs and masters it fairly well before he ventures to take up the succeeding part. When he finishes the entire lesson, he is convinced that having mastered well each individual part, he has just as thoroughly mastered the whole. Such a method, indeed, may have the advantage of insuring a relatively permanent retention of certain details. But it fails to achieve a very important thing— *perspective.* Since all the items have been conscientiously learned as if they were of equal importance, the student is left with a mass of data without the lights and shadows. There will be little appreciation of the relative importance between parts. High spots will not stand out in relief. Correlation between parts will have escaped him. The various sections of the lesson have come into his mind in a piecemeal fashion and are likely to remain there in a state of detachment, whereas they should settle down into a well-knit, logical unit. But what good is a bundle of facts unless the relationship between them is comprehended?

Both of these methods have the same serious defect: the student has closed his lesson without really turning his mental powers loose and without setting his mind to work upon the material. He has merely crowded his mind with a batch of facts without attempting to establish perspective between them, or to detect any hidden implications or to draw any conclusions of his own. In other words, he has not risen, nor made any attempt to rise, to intellectual mastery. Consequently, when he is confronted with a list of examination questions which demand more than mere information, he is startled by their novelty. Returning to the same material after the examination is over, he is surprised to see what he has missed.

"LONG-RANGE" METHOD

The "long-range" method with questions and answers is better than either of these two. It consists of four steps. The first step is to read over the entire lesson thoughtfully, taking mental notice of the relatively important points. But there is no pausing or retracing, except, perhaps, when required to ascertain the sense of certain difficult passages. But even in such exceptional cases, if the sense is not bared by a slight pause or after one or two retracings, the student continues without further interruptions and without any uneasiness over his failure to understand certain parts. This part of the process is progressive and fairly rapid, moving straight forward through the assignment from beginning to end. Its purpose is to give a bird's-eye view of the whole matter. It furnishes a kind of rough map of the entire text and should reveal the relatively important parts and some of the significant relationships existing between them.

The second step is deliberate rereading, section by section, aiming for complete mastery. To achieve this mastery, formulate a question or two bearing directly upon the essential content of each section. Any given paragraph, for instance, must or should unfold one dominating thought. Whatever that dominating thought is, turn it into a direct question. Set the question down on paper. Never mind if it looks strange. Your question is a challenge to the text. Then set down the answer to the question, not in full, but briefly, in outline form and always in your own words. Pay as little attention as possible to the phraseology or style of the author. Remember *you* are attacking the matter. Merely repeating the words of another is not learning. The matter must be grasped by *your* mind. Your goal is to think the thing through and to understand it, no matter how awkward the process may seem. Your answer, then, will be a summary and a record of the material you have actually learned. The greater part of the study period should be devoted to this second step of critical analysis.

The third step is reviewing your own summary to clinch the material in your mind and at the same time to perceive the relationships between the various parts. Ask questions of yourself and demand answers, checking and repeating the whole process until the matter is thoroughly established in your mind. This is merely an application of overlearning which should never be lost sight of. (Cf. Chapter VII.)

These three steps in learning may be compared to the three steps required in drawing a map. In making a map, you first sketch the general outline and set down the principal or outstanding parts. Then you proceed to fill in the less important parts until the map has reached the stage of completion desired. Finally, you sit back and scrutinize the map in its completed form. You really have not learned a thing well, unless you have "mapped" it in your mind, i.e., grasped the matter as a whole with all its parts arranged in order.

The fourth step is to reread the original assignment as rapidly as possible to catch any significant facts or relationships which might have previously escaped unnoticed. This step is a quick final checkup in the interest of completeness and exactness. It is not essential, but the brief time it requires is time well invested.

The advantages of this "long-range" method will be more apparent to you if you once try it. It puts you in a challenging, aggressive mood, which makes the process of study an interesting venture. Your powers of concentration are raised to a high level, and the habit of discrimination and analysis is fostered. Easier retention and thorough mastery result. Your own questions and answers, although they may seem awkward, give you the conviction that you are really doing something and making headway.

The method has one disadvantage. It requires mental exertion. But this is exactly what studying should be. Merely letting someone else's thoughts pass through your mind is not thinking. It is only a substitute for thinking. Studying should provoke original thought.

However, there are certain cautions that must be noted. The method described should not be used on assignments that are extremely long. It works best on assignments which can be read through in an hour or less. A general rule is that your mind should still be fresh and active after you have completed the first step of rapid reading from beginning to end. Assignments of greater length should be broken down into units convenient to handle. Then each unit may be treated separately as described above.

Common sense suggests that the method, after a fair trial, be modified to suit the matter under treatment. Not all subjects can be learned by the same technique. The method is advised only for those subjects which are principally informative. It may not work as well with mathematics. It should work well for history, English, economics, sociology and possibly philosophy. You may discover that you are able to use the method well without using a pencil as suggested. But do not be too hasty in dispensing with the pencil. A pencil is a marvelous little prodder of thought.

Give the method a fair trial. But always feel free to modify it. Any system of study should make you the master of the situation and not put you in chains.

REPETITION

I am here referring to repetition not as the means to memorize a thing but as the means to learn it in the first place.

There are certain matters which are ordinarily understood as soon as the mind has carefully attended to them. A history lesson, for instance, may be difficult to remember, but usually it is not hard to understand. But a lesson in mathematics, philosophy or chemistry belongs to another class. It requires a different kind of attack. Here it is not the remembering of it that gives you difficulty, but the initial understanding of it. You may go over a certain lesson very thoughtfully and completely without succeeding in grasping it mentally. The matter is such that it seems to resist your best effort to understand or assimilate it.

This should not surprise or discourage you. Some things are in themselves more difficult to grasp, for any mind, than others. To understand them you must be willing to pay the price. *Some things should not be expected to be fully grasped at once.* Their understanding does not burst like a rocket but dawns like a slow sunrise. Their mastery requires more than one mental application. Realize this truth now and you will save yourself a great deal of disappointment and discouragement.

These things require more than concentrated study. They require *repeated study.* The identical matter must be studied thoroughly and carefully again and again. It must be attacked several times, each time with the same force and concentration. Be satisfied if difficulties melt away slowly. Each attack will yield a better understanding. What seemed to be impossible to learn at first finally becomes clear by gradual degrees. The intervals between the separate study periods give your subconscious mind an opportunity to expend itself. When you return to the matter again, you harvest the results of the operation of your subconscious mind, which has been at work quietly and without effort. It is really interesting to experience how difficulties and perplexities gradually dissolve if you only give yourself time.

This, of course, requires patience, which is the better part of industry. So if your assignment in philosophy or mathematics is not grasped after one sound study period of normal length, quietly and good naturedly lay it away for another time. You must be patient enough to return to it again. This is the only way some things are *ever* learned. Impatient expectation of quick results in learning destroys composure, leads quickly to discouragement and robs us of many fine intellectual acquisitions.

STUDY FAST

This does not mean that you should be in constant haste or in a state of nervous rush. It means that a given job should be done with a minimum expenditure of time by bearing down resolutely on the matter at hand with all the stops of the mind wide open and eliminating all distractions and side-tracking occupations. It takes time to warm up to any intellectual work. This is to be expected, but don't dally about in lackadaisical fashion hopefully waiting to be touched by some sudden and mysterious inspiration. The initial period of any intellectual work is likely to be dull and laborious. But when the time of interest and full energy arrives, drive through the matter smoothly at top speed. There should be rest periods, of course, but these should be planned with deliberation and not as easy surrenders to distractions or weak concessions to mental sloth. Work steadily, even though the work period itself is brief.

If by smooth, efficient application you can do in fifty minutes what you ordinarily do in sixty minutes, you have made a sixteen-percent saving in time. If the same percentage of timesaving is extended to all your studying, you are strides ahead of your former record of performance. The time saved may mean that you are always abreast of your work requirements, or perhaps have extra time for reviewing or for attention to personal and social matters.

This does not imply that time is saved at the expense of accuracy and thoroughness. Take all the time that is needed to be accurate and thorough, but don't divide your actual study time between intellectual work and irrelevant occupations. Study time should be, whenever possible, an unbroken, mental application whether the period be long or short.

Such a method of study not only eliminates a needless waste of time, but it is actually conducive to better work. Thoughts move swiftly. When a given amount of work is traversed rapidly, the connecting links between the parts are better understood, and one part learned immediately contributes to the understanding of other parts. Momentum is gained without impairment of understanding.

LEARN BY WRITING

If, while thinking hard over a subject you are tempted to seize a pencil and write down your thoughts, give the impulse free play. Many people are tempted to write out their thoughts but allow their self-consciousness to stifle the inspiration. Your thoughts on paper are singularly your own. Even to write ten connected sentences on a given subject requires a great deal of concentration and original thought. Writing is almost sure to reveal great defects and gaps in your knowledge —sometimes in a manner which is quite startling. A thought struggling for light is often assisted by the mere attempt to write it. Many thoughts and answers to problems dwell vaguely in the twilight until some definite attempt to express them pushes them into the full light of understanding. It is surprising how some things clarify themselves and widen out into other associations and implications when written.

This is particularly true of all matter which requires intellectual penetration, for instance, in understanding a difficult definition, in following the trend of a complicated argument or in mastering any material in which the parts fit together in logical sequence. Philosophy, mathematics, problems in physics and chemistry, etc., are fields where these suggestions are of special value.

In writing a thing out in order to understand it better, it is not necessary to write it out in full. A schematized summary will often be sufficient. Sentences need not be complete. It is only necessary that the writing carry the thought along a definite channel. If full sentences are used they should aim at compression, not beauty. If diagrams, geometrical figures or pictures suggest themselves as expressing or illustrating a thought, use them without too much concern about their crudeness. You are merely trying to express the thought for your own understanding.

LEARN BY SPEAKING

Everyone knows by his own experience how thought is stimulated and clarified by the mere effort to tell another what he knows. New thoughts are born every time we attempt to unfold our own thoughts seriously to another. A pertinent question interposed here and there is often sufficient to set the whole matter in a different light, suggest a new approach, bring up new illustrations or recast the method of explanation. How often have we begun to explain a thing uncertain of our ability or uncertain of our knowledge of the subject, only to be surprised at our own success. But at other times, attempts at oral explanation make us quickly and acutely aware that we lack the necessary knowledge and understanding which all along we had imagined ourselves to possess. But there is gain in such honest failures. They shatter the all-too-common illusion of personal wisdom and drive us back to our books or other sources of information to supply the deficiencies which we have been forced to acknowledge. Writing our thoughts on paper certainly primes the mind to original effort. But in speaking there is the exhilaration of actual contact of mind with mind. And for this there is no substitute. The advantage of oral instruction or of a quiet discussion on a serious topic is that it invites our best and deepest thinking without making us conscious of the effort. It is one of the most natural and efficient methods of learning.

All this is common knowledge. Yet how few students employ speech as a method of learning. Abbe Dimnet, in *The Art of Thinking*, tells of two men who succeeded in making their months in prison without book, pen or paper a profitable intellectual experience (pp. 151-52). Each day they would go over what they remembered about a definite subject. One day it would be history, another day philosophy and another day literature. They pooled their knowledge, each trying to supplement what the other had forgotten. It was a veritable contact of mind with mind, and the prisoners became student and teacher to each other.

Sometimes opportunities of serious oral discussion, which may serve to clarify thought or to consolidate data which you have already learned, come to you without being sought. There are recitations, for instance. They are ready-made opportunities for learning and thinking. For the greatest value of a recitation is not that it enables the instructor to probe your knowledge, but that it draws from you the effort to tell what you know or to utilize your knowledge, thus exposing you to the necessity of deeper thought. Haven't you ever discovered that you have actually learned something quite new by the mere attempt to recite? Every recitation is a challenge to thought. Or have you ever been asked to coach a fellow student? Or to explain to him a lesson or a number of lessons which he has missed or failed to understand? Here are golden opportunities for you to put your thoughts into words and to teach yourself by teaching others. Be alert to recognize such opportunities when they occur and utilize them to their fullest extent for your own improvement.

At other times you may create such opportunities more or less deliberately. It is remarkable what two students, both interested in their work, can do by recounting to each other what they have learned, one taking one subject and the other another subject. A quiet discussion on some topic of history or some problem in philosophy is an excellent way for two minds to meet and sharpen each other's understanding. Regularity at such informal conversations will inevitably beget familiarity with many subjects which are almost forbidden topics outside the classroom and the textbook. It takes away the character of bookishness which hangs over so much of our knowledge. Does this seem strange and pedantic? But why shouldn't two people meet for the sole purpose of thinking?

Have you just completed an interesting book, finished reading an entry in the encyclopedia or returned from a lecture? Why not turn the matter over again in your mind by recounting it for someone else who may be interested but does not have the same opportunity to learn it? A thing told is a thing relearned. Such informal oral reviews of a book or lecture are merely another practical way of overlearning. (Cf. Chapter VII.) How many valuable books, which we have not read and will not ever be able to read, would pour their riches upon us if we would break down our mental isolation and establish an intellectual liaison between our own and other kindred, congenial minds. Imagine how much any two people could learn, one from the other, merely by swapping the contents of the books which they happen to read!

Have you ever made the discovery that you can often master an abstruse problem or a difficult lesson by talking the matter over and aloud with yourself? Try it. Some of the best philosophers of the world, Plato and Saint Augustine for example, have recorded their thoughts in the form of dialogue. They simply wrote as they talked to themselves. Talking a matter over with yourself is merely an unwritten dialogue. It is done best by imagining vividly that there is an interested listener present who is anxious to hear what you have to say or who is prone to dispute your word. You are then not just talking to yourself, but to a second person who is an imagined ear witness to your thoughts. Again do not be too self-conscious. Let yourself go. When you are talking a matter over with yourself in order to learn it, you are merely employing speech as an instrument of thought. It is just as sensible to "talk a thing out," even to yourself, as it is to "write it out." When you are thus talking to or with yourself, you are really thinking and, by thinking, learning.

At any rate, be alert to seize or to create opportunities to turn your thoughts, knowledge and problems into your own speech. Such speech, however, should remain definitely above the level of light conversation. It should be serious speech in the direction of a goal. Aim to explain the matter under treatment laconically and succinctly. Practice getting a thing said with the fewest possible number of words. A voluble flow of words is likely to drown the exact point of an argument or the thought of a sentence. The effort to secure economy in the use of words stimulates thought, and the art once achieved is a sure mark of a thinker.

Suggestions

1. Try the "long-range" method. Do you think that it is practical?
2. What are the implications in the following statements:
   a. To learn a lesson well one must do a little mental "backtalk."
   b. One does not know a thing thoroughly unless he can tell it in words of one syllable.
3. How does impatience for quick results hinder thorough learning?
4. Unfold to one who is patient enough to listen the contents of the last book you have read. What are the advantages of such a process?
5. What opportunities can you create for telling, teaching or using material which you have learned?

CHAPTER IX

Taking Notes

A college student soon learns that taking notes is a necessity of daily recurrence. In collecting material for themes and term papers, reporting on research reading and taking memoranda of class lectures, some kind of note taking becomes indispensable. Lecture courses, which require no textbook in class, make your success absolutely dependent on the right kind of notes. In only a few classes, such as elementary language courses and those which merely require the mastery of a single textbook, can note taking be dispensed with. The present chapter deals with the question of note taking, which is required in connection with class lectures, although the general principles and suggestions presented will apply, with modifications, to note taking of any kind.

ADVANTAGES OF TAKING NOTES

The purpose of taking notes? No student would hesitate to answer: "They supply a reliable memorandum of the matter treated in class and thus serve as an essential aid for passing examinations." Indeed, most students settle down to the task of note taking for the sole purpose of putting the matter "on ice" till the day of examination. Notes taken in class do and should serve this useful purpose. But your notebook is much more than a textbook personally compiled for future reference.

The chief benefit of taking notes is that it aids the process of learning. While you are taking notes you are actually learning the matter. Class attendance should not be a patient, passive process of listening to a lecture. Little is learned and little is remembered by mere audition. It is the vigorous, active cooperation and mental reaction to the matter presented that usually counts. While you are taking notes, even though poorly, you are alert; you are concentrating, distinguishing incidentals from essentials, watching for points and proofs and marking as best you can the general drift of the explanation. You are doing something mentally. You are attacking the matter. This kind of mental attitude means that you are learning. Here the advantage lies not so much in the set of notes which you carry out of the classroom with you, as in the actual process of taking notes.

The actual taking of notes also has the incidental but very important benefit of aiding the memory to retain the matter thus treated. The eyes and tactual senses are being employed to reinforce and deepen the impressions. Writing a thing out, even though it may not help you to understand, always helps you to remember. The traveler who keeps a diary will remember more about a journey than one who does not. An experience which he has written down will be more easily remembered just because he has noted it, even though he may never look at the record which he made. Your set of notes is like a diary, "a record of an intellectual voyage, containing reference to all important events and points covered."* The mere fact that you have written down the matter will help to make it stick. Even though your notes were lost or destroyed, leaving you with no memorandum to review for examination, they will have fulfilled a worthwhile and valuable purpose.

REQUIREMENTS FOR TAKING GOOD NOTES

All this may not be appreciated by the inexperienced note taker. For many college students, taking notes is just another laborious, tedious process which turns out to be a disappointment even as an aid for passing examinations. Ordinarily a college student turns out a poor set of notes. They are too sketchy or too verbose. They may represent a futile attempt to record verbatim practically everything that the lecturer said, in which case the note taker has nothing for his pains but a loose string of random statements without order or connection which baffle understanding when he turns to use them. If your notes result in confusion and disappointment when you turn to study them, it is a sure indication that the task has been poorly done. But it is never too late or too early to learn how to take good notes.

There are five requirements for taking a good set of notes:

1. You must first *grasp the substance* of the lecture, i.e., comprehend the general drift of the thought.
2. You must record the substance comprehended in a *logical order.*
3. You must make the record *complete*, i.e., including whatever is essential,
4. and *concise*, i.e., excluding whatever is unessential,
5. and *in your own words* whenever possible.

---

*Jones, *Improvement of Study Habits*, p. 21.

GRASPING THE SUBSTANCE

Grasping the substance of a lecture is an intellectual exercise of the highest order. It means that the mind is at work on the matter of the spoken word, analyzing, differentiating and sorting out the points before the pen is put to paper. It is easier to tell you to get the substance of a lecture than to tell you exactly how to do it. However, there are a few general principles and hints which might help.

Remember that every good lecture develops a main theme which can usually be expressed in one complete sentence or proposition. It is a unit consisting of logical divisions and subdivisions which fit together and should be understood as a whole. There is a progression from point to point, a movement from one train of thought to another, until a circuit is completed. There may be digressions and interruptions, sometimes deliberately inserted to relieve tension. Frequently there are anecdotes and illustrations to clarify a point. But the movement of a good lecture is always toward a goal. You must distinguish clearly in your mind where a digression begins and ends and where the thread of argument is resumed. You must also differentiate between a given point and the illustration or anecdote which clarifies it. To laugh at a humorous anecdote, for instance, and miss the point which the anecdote is meant to clarify indicates a failure to discriminate. In fact, a humorous anecdote may illustrate a very serious thought so that one may be more inclined to meditate than to laugh. In this case it would be better to forget the humor of the anecdote and nail down the point, than to remember the anecdote and miss the point.

There may be an accumulation of illustrations all serving to clarify the same idea. Or there may be repetitions and planned rephrasings of the same thought. Good lecturers do this frequently to make sure that the whole class gets the point or to impress the class with its importance. You should be alert to realize when there is a pause in the forward movement of the lecture due to repetitions. If you have caught the point clearly when it was first expressed or illustrated, you may safely ignore other expressions and illustrations of the same thought. It is time now to give your pen and notebook a rest till the drift of the discussion turns and moves onward. Get the feel of onward movement of the theme and note only the points or items which carry it forward.

Be on the alert for transitions of thought. If you cannot tell where and when the current of treatment shifts its direction, the substance of the matter is eluding your grasp. Certain phrases and words indicate a change of thought, e.g., "moreover," "in addition to this," "however," "on the contrary," "secondly," "finally," etc. If the instructor should say,

"Now there are three reasons for this assertion," you know at once that you ought to have the gist of the assertion written in your notebook and that there are three distinct items to be classified under it. Some lecturers are dramatic and like to indicate a fresh turn of thought by a long pause, by lowering the voice, etc. Other lecturers are rapid in the sense that they set forth their points rather nakedly without the usual warning of transitional phrases or sentences. But at all time you must be able to discern where one item of importance finishes and another begins.

Of course, much depends on the method and ability of the lecturer. If he never hits the track firmly and never seems to push the train of ideas ahead to a definite goal, you will have to discover the track and the goal the best you can and thus supply his deficiency. Some lecturers are easy to follow. Their lectures bear sensible and significant titles; introductions trace out in advance the main divisions of the subject; recapitulations at the end help to tie everything together and perhaps supply points which you may have missed; blackboard outlines before you map out the voyage of thought, indicating the points which lie ahead; the whole presentation is systematic and clear; new points and turns of thought click distinctly; and there is the impression that the thought is developing. Moreover, such lecturers may patiently tolerate interruptions from students asking questions or requesting repetitions and additional information. If you have such an instructor, you know that he is earning his salary and will have little difficulty getting at the substance of his lecture.

But there are certain things that you ought to do, regardless of the competence of the lecturer. You should get the correct title of the lecture. This will indicate the theme. There is an advantage in writing out titles in the form of questions. For instance, instead of writing "Causes of the French Revolution," write "What caused the French Revolution?" or "Why did the French revolt?" A title written down in the form of a question creates a stimulating challenge to thought. Having the title down on paper, do not write a single word in the body of your notes unless it seems to answer the question. When the notes are finished, they should furnish you with a satisfactory answer. If they do not, you have failed to grasp the argument of the discussion.

If the lecturer gives you a general outline of the lesson or writes one on the blackboard, be sure to take it down. Blackboard outlines are very useful in getting at the essential development of the theme. But remember that the lecturer's outline is his own and will have to be modified and supplemented considerably before it will be of maximum value for you.

There may be a general resume or a recapitulation of the whole matter at the end of the lecture. Watch for these recapitulations. If they agree closely with what you already have down in your notes, there is nothing further for you to do. But ordinarily a good recapitulation will indicate certain omissions and faults in your notes which are to be corrected then and there. Every recapitulatory passage in the lecture is an opportunity for you to check your comprehension of the matter and to test the essential completeness of your notes.

NOTES SHOULD BE ORDERLY

The work of comprehending the substance of a lecture and its logical development is entirely an intellectual performance. The next thing to do is to get what you understand down on paper. When you begin to set down notes in your notebook, do so *in order*. This means that each of the main points will stand out prominently as distinct divisions of thought, with all the supporting ideas and facts arranged under their respective headings. In other words, items should be recorded in such a way as to indicate their mutual relationships. The way to achieve this is to record your notes in the form of an outline, making use of indentations. The purpose of an indentation is to furnish a visual aid to show the coordination and subordination of the various parts, i.e., to show how the different points rank in reference to each other.

Pages 89 and 90 show a sample outline of the first part of this chapter. Study it carefully and see for yourself what is meant by recording notes in logical order by using a system of indentation. On the sample pages of notes the student has recorded four main ideas, viz., the "necessity," "benefits," "defects" and "requirements" of a good set of notes. These are distinct aspects of the subject, and to show this distinction he has set them down separately and labeled each with a roman numeral (I, II, III, IV). He has expressed each of these leading thoughts in the form of a question. Under each "leader" come the ideas which are subordinate to it. Their subordinate character is clear at a glance because he has not only written them under the "leader" but also further to the right of the margin and has labeled them differently by using capital letters. When such subordinate ideas are further supported or developed by others, these others are written on separate lines below and still further to the right of the margin and again marked differently, this time by arabic numerals (1, 2, 3). Whenever an idea is written on a line below another and indented further to the right, it is an indication of logical subordination. Thus all the essential points are not only set down, but they are set down in their proper position and rank and in a way which clearly indicates the relationship which exists between them. The ideas are not only recorded, but they are sorted out and put into a system. A good outline, then, is not an attempted essay or a stringy summary and is considerably more than a mere abridgment. It is a logical graph.

It is seldom necessary to make more than two or three indentations under any given heading. If the writer of the sample outline given should have needed further indentations below those marked with arabic numerals, he could have marked these with small letters (a, b, c). Further indentations will be rarely, if ever, needed. But if they should be required, the labeling may begin all over again, starting with roman numerals. But labeling the main headings and their respective divisions and subdivisions of thought is a matter of minor importance. A good outline, especially a brief one, may get along quite well without any labels. Almost any system of marking will do, provided it is used consistently throughout the entire outline. The important thing is the system of indentation.

In using the outline system it is well to express the main headings in the form of complete statements or in the form of questions. Try to word the statement or the question so that all of it will fit on one line. Once the outline is started, do not add anything unless it represents a new thought or some further development. Whatever is added should have some logical relationship to whatever has been already written down and in a way which shows what this relationship is. When you get into divisions and subdivisions, always look for a chance to get back to the left of the page as soon as possible.

Pages 89 and 90 are samples of outlines or note taking which were actually taken by two different students who once attended the author's lecture on this subject. It is apparent that student A, who made the first outline presented on page 89, had not been merely listening and copying what he heard. His outline shows analysis and originality. The use of indentations makes the order of the thoughts stand out, and everything put down stands related to something else. The whole thing is a nice logical unit. Moreover, you can easily understand that once he has made the outline, he has the matter practically learned. With thought linked to thought the work of remembering the matter is reduced to a minimum and the task of subsequent review is comparatively easy.

None of these advantages will be shared by student B, who turned in the random notes presented on pages 89 and 90. Student B simply cut into the lecture wherever he could and jotted down as many facts and arguments as he could write, but without any mental effort to sift and correlate them. No logical linkage is apparent. The result is a loose string of random statements without order and, hence, difficult to comprehend or remember. It is evident that in compiling such notes his pencil was busier than his mind.

Notes in the Form of an Orderly Outline

I When are notes required
    A) In theme writing, term papers, lecture courses, research reading etc.
    B) Not necessary in mere Text, Bk courses, v.g. elementary German.

II What benefits should I expect from notes?
    A) Handy review for exams – <u>not</u> the most important.
    B) Assists actual learning. You are learning while you take notes, because –
        1) it requires attention, concentration etc.
        2) " stimulates discrimination, search for essentials vs. incidentals.
    C) Aids memory. because –
        1) eyes & tactual senses at work – better than just listening.
        2) writing a thing helps to pin it down, e.g diary.

III Why are notes often disappointing?
    A) Too brief & sketchy.
    B) " verbose, nearly everything recorded.
    C) No order – mere random series

IV What is required for a good set of notes?
    A) You must grasp the substance, get the drift
    B) Record completely, i.e. <u>all</u> essentials.
    C) " concisely, i.e. <u>no</u> unessentials.
    D) " in order, make whole matter a <u>systematic</u> unit

Notes in the Form of a Random Series

Necessary to take notes for themes, making term papers, class lectures, etc. Especially in lecture courses – no text book used. Not necessary in German course – use text book. Fine for reviews & exams. Puts things on ice. Helps you to learn — Don't merely listen in class. Makes you concentrate. Know essentials and unessentials. — Gets reaction. Helps memory — man makes diary on trip, remembers more about his vacation. Why? — Too many poor notes — Students know how — Notes sketchy, verbatim, no order. No good. Just loose string — Are your notes confusing, disappointing? Learn to make good notes — necessary to get substance of lecture. Drift of thought. Logical order, system. Take in everything essential. Notes concise? No unessential matter. Don't just copy. Use own words. Requirement for good notes.

Suggestions

1. Has the study of this chapter modified your idea concerning the purpose and value of note taking?
2. Are you sure that you understand the difference between coordinate and subordinate ideas? Examine the first outline on page 89 and distinguish the coordinate from the subordinate statements.
3. Critically examine a page or two of your notebook. Are your notes easy to read? Are they satisfactory for review? Detect your own defects.
4. Rearrange the same material and organize it into a logical outline as suggested in this chapter. Note the improvement.
5. At your next opportunity of taking notes in class, try to make as perfect a set of notes as possible, using the system of indentation to indicate thought relationships. What is the principal difficulty of taking notes in this way? Is it in the mechanical business of taking down the notes or in the mental effort required to relate thought to thought?
6. Do you find it easier to take notes in some classes than in others? Is this due to the nature of the matter treated or to the instructor's manner of presentation?

CHAPTER X

More on Taking Notes

Once you seriously attempt to understand the substance of the lecture and set this down in an orderly outline, as indicated in the previous chapter, your notes will begin to take on the character of completeness and conciseness. The indented outline style of notes is an automatic step toward this goal.

COMPLETENESS

Your record is complete when it includes all the essential items which constitute the theme of the lecture. At first, the task of getting all the essentials of a lecture in your notebook may seem to be an impossible achievement. The student may state his case: "It's easy for the instructor to talk, but I have to follow the spoken word with the pencil. The spoken word is faster than the written word. I have to catch things on the run, and while I am getting one thing down in my notebook, the spoken discourse has gone on to another point which I am compelled to miss. I am handicapped in an uneven race, plodding away with my pencil while the spoken word glides on. How can my notes be anything but fragmentary and incomplete?"

Of course, it is much easier to make a satisfactory outline of a book than a lecture. In analyzing the written word, there are the conveniences of artificial aids, like paragraphing, headings, italics, etc. The written word stands still and patiently submits to prolonged scrutiny and any number of rereadings. It allows you all the time which you are willing to expend on it. But no one expects your lecture outlines to be as neat and complete as a book analysis.

But there is something about a lecture which favors the note taker. The spoken word, especially in a classroom lecture, is more verbose, more padded with irrelevancies and redundancies than the written word. The very ease of speaking, in contrast with the slow labor of writing, invites verbosity and rhetorical ornamentation. Moreover, in a good classroom lecture there are numerous repetitions and perhaps several illustrations serving to clarify a single point—all of which are deliberately planned so that the matter will be grasped by the various types of minds represented in the class. A lecturer may also introduce irrelevant anecdotes and dashes of humor and off-the-record remarks as a kind of salutary lubrication to keep the grind out of the work and to put the class in a good humor. No classroom lecturer dares risk a crisp, trenchant, concise style of treatment which might be admirably suited to a book or an essay. This simplifies the work of taking notes. There is never any necessity of taking down everything a lecturer says. There is always plenty of irrelevant and repetitious matter. If you catch the point with the first illustration, put down the point with an abbreviated reference to the illustration. If there are further illustrations and anecdotes to bring out the same point, never mind about getting these down in your notebook. They are for other members of the class who might have missed the point of the first one. Discriminate between the irrelevant and the relevant, between the first statement of a fact and subsequent restatements. Take down only what is relevant and what is necessary for understanding and ignore with pleasure everything else. Usually there will be sufficient time and seldom is there any need for desperate rushing, even if the pen is slower than the spoken word. "Making notes is like playing tennis in that the novice always has more time for receiving than he thinks he has."* The job of taking notes is more a matter of intellectual discrimination between essentials and incidentals than a rush of writing against time.

"Should a student take down the lecture in shorthand if he is able to do so?" This is surely one way to secure completeness. But there are special reasons why stenographic lecture notes would not be desirable, even though they would guarantee absolute completeness. In making a stenographic report of a lecture, there is little attention given to a critical analysis of the matter, which is after all the thing that means learning. A good stenographer will copy a lecture without thinking about the matter at all. It is words that he gets and not ideas. Thus the process of taking notes loses its principal advantage of being an *aid to learning.* A note-taking student should be a student who is at work on the matter.

Moreover, a stenographic report must be decoded and typed—more mechanical labor—but requires no actual intellectual effort to understand. Finally, when the report is completed it will include all the irrelevant and miscellaneous material of the lecture which will be nothing but an annoyance when it comes time to study and review it. Thus completeness has been secured but at the expense of conciseness.

---

*Headley, *How to Study in College,* p. 329.

CONCISENESS

Conciseness demands the elimination of unessentials, the sure mark of a trained thinker. Many students have no time to gather up all the essentials because they are too much occupied getting down unessentials. Two kinds of unessentials are likely to appear in your notes: matter which is purely repetitious and matter which is extraneous to the subject. This distinction paves the way for two simple rules for achieving conciseness or precision.

1. Avoid repetitions, even though they are relevant. Once a point is down on paper, there is no use of writing it down again. If one illustration serves to elucidate a point for you, there is no use of adding a second and a third. "Very simple and true," you say! Then look at your notes and see what an overload of repetitious material they carry. Repetitions and restatements consume time in writing and add no value to your notes. Your notes are richer in value if they are lean of repetitious matter.

2. Resolutely avoid extraneous material, at least in the body of your outline. While lecturing, I have often noticed students racing their pencils across their notebooks in feverish haste while there is nothing of importance being said. This frequently happens during the preliminary remarks introducing a lecture. Some lecturers say absolutely nothing worthy of note during the first two or three minutes. They are merely making pleasant remarks till the class settles down, or endeavoring to put the auditors in an agreeable state of mind. Or perhaps they are doing a little verbal sparring just to get warmed up. If you notice that the instructor customarily takes a few minutes to get himself warmed up to the subject, let him do it. But keep your pencil at rest till he hits his stride and gets into the matter. But if your instructor is one who is quick on the start and plunges directly into the subject, you will have to be prepared to take notes from the start.

Put nothing into your outline unless it belongs there. If it does not advance the theme or the argument of the case, it has no place in your notes. Test everything by relevancy and the result will be conciseness. The whole case of conciseness rests with your ability to recognize what is to be eliminated.

DOUBLE-ENTRY SYSTEM OF NOTES

There may be a danger in exacting too much conciseness. Conciseness excludes irrelevancy. But an irrelevant thought, while not adding to the development of the central theme, may nevertheless be a valuable thought worth recording. It just happens to be irrelevant. In every lecture there is a certain amount of miscellaneous, irrelevant material like anecdotes, humorous allusions, interesting digressions, off-the-record comments by the professor, reading references and original observations made by the student himself. If such miscellaneous material is padded into the outline, it would be seriously encumbered and thrown out of gear. But still some of it may be worthy of record. If the miscellaneous material is slight and occasional, it may be inserted into the outline but enclosed within brackets or parentheses. This would indicate its irrelevant character and still not scramble the outline.

I would strongly advise, however, what may be called the "double-entry" system of notes. It consists of using only the left page of your notebook for entering the regular outlines and leaving the right page free. This free page to the right of the outline will give you several advantages. On this page you will have plenty of space to write down whatever miscellaneous matter you decide is worth recording, without any danger of cluttering your outline. When such entries are made they should be made directly to the right of the section of the outline to which they refer. It may also be used to record your own observations, illustrations, reactions and questions. It is a suitable place to insert any additional data or information which you may gather from collateral reading. Sometimes it may be used for revising your outline if necessary. Such a "double-entry" system catches whatever additional matter you may desire to record and at the same time leaves your outline free of encumbrances, an advantage which you will appreciate when the time comes to review.

RECORDING IN YOUR OWN WORDS

Record the matter in your notes in your own words whenever possible. Your notebook is not a copy book or reliquary of borrowed statements. Make your notes your own. Once an idea is in your mind, it derives additional clarity by the attempt to express it. Writing is a clarifier of thought. I do not believe that any idea becomes thoroughly our own until we command it so completely that we are able to express it in our own words. Ignoring the value of original expression of thought is an invitation to mediocrity. The words of the lecturer are merely his way of expressing his thoughts to you. They are not intended as a model for you to express your own thoughts.

However, there are exceptions to this general rule. There are many times when a brief verbatim report is required, for instance, in recording definitions, quotations and certain concise proofs which you will want to scrutinize later at your leisure. But where there is no need to have such an exact record, be as original as you can. The circumstances of taking notes in class naturally do not allow much time for independent reflection needed for original writing. But never feel that you are bound to write everything down exactly as the professor says it. If you must write it that way do so, but if another way suggests itself to your mind, do not hesitate to express it that way. If an original example or anecdote occurs to you, write it down in preference to any other. Originality in taking notes means that you are bearing down on the matter with all your intellectual energy and will give you a record which will have value and vitality quite superior to the mere copy book of the passive, imitative scribe.

DIFFICULTIES

When the inexperienced note taker first sets out to outline a lecture in class, the first difficulty he encounters is that it requires a considerable amount of concentration and intellectual alertness. It makes you think. But this is just the reason why you should undertake it. There is no other way to master a subject but by hard thinking. I do not recommend the system because it is easy, but because it is one way to learn. Naturally no set of notes taken in class will be perfect. Never mind if your outline is somewhat faulty. The very attempt to make one has stimulated the processes of analytical thought and has made you attack the matter with a vigorous initiative. Even a faulty outline is far superior, from almost every point of view, to any other kind of class notes. With a little practice, however, the performance will improve. It is only the beginning that is especially difficult.

Sometimes a special difficulty may arise from the nature of the lecture itself. In certain subjects the lecturer proceeds from specific points to general conclusions. He unfolds his subject gradually but keeps the main idea waiting as a climax at the end. In such a procedure it is impossible to know the main idea or general goal of the discussion until it is actually reached. You may, of course, anticipate what it will be. In such cases there is only one thing to do—put down the different steps in their logical sequence and wait till you discover the general goal or conclusion to which they lead. When this is discovered, go back in your notes and put it down as a main heading above the items which you already have recorded. In this case, "the last shall be first."

Occasionally a difficulty may arise from the incompetence of the lecturer himself. He may talk too fast. He may deliver the matter in such a random, unsystematic manner, or so whisker the sense of even obvious things with unnecessary verbal cant, or so encumber his sentences with structural complexities that it is practically impossible to make head or tail out of what he says. My advice is to avoid taking the classes of such instructors whenever possible. But if such instructors are simply unavoidable, you will have to take notes the best you can and attend to organizing them later.

REVISING NOTES

Some writers on this subject suggest that your classroom notes should always be rewritten. This advice seems to me to be extreme. Do not start your notes with the assumption that they will need to be rewritten. Rather take the attitude that they are to be done so well in the first place that rewriting them will not be necessary. Of course, sometimes, especially in the beginning or in a matter of unusual difficulty, your notes on a given lecture will be so faulty and confused that they ought to be completely overhauled. If so, rewrite them in their entirety and throw the original notes away. Ordinarily, your notes will need some revisions. There may be minor additions and corrections to make, or you may discover that certain items have been written in the wrong places, perhaps under the wrong headings. If you find that a certain portion is not in its logical place, it is not always necessary to cross it out and rewrite it in its correct position. Just leave it stand where it is and draw an arrow pointing to the place where it ought to be. Thus a certain number of corrections can be made without erasing or rewriting. Notes corrected in this way will not be patterns of neatness, but they will still serve their purpose.

Whatever the kind of revision is required, it is important to make it as soon after the class period as possible. For the work of revision is much easier while the memory of the lecture is still fresh.

Since most of your lecture notes, or perhaps nearly all of them, will need a little repair work, anticipate this need while you are drafting them in class. Make your original notes a little elastic so that they may easily receive future minor corrections and revisions without being crowded. This can be done by leaving generous spaces between the main headings and smaller but usable spaces between the subdivisions. You may not need these free spaces, but they are there if you do.

GENERAL SUGGESTIONS

1. There are advantages to using one notebook for all classes. Besides the convenience of having one notebook to carry about instead of

two or more, you eliminate the danger of turning up for chemistry with your history notebook under your arm.

2. There is a special convenience to using a looseleaf notebook. Certain pages can be removed and replaced by better copies. Additional pages bearing pertinent material gathered from research reading can be added. It may be helpful to have the various parts pertaining to different subjects separated by colored construction paper or thin card board.

3. Large-sized paper, 8½ by 11, is preferable to smaller sizes. A page of ample size allows plenty of room for large writing and gives plenty of space for four or five indentations. A tiny notebook may be dainty and more convenient to put into your pocket and carry around, but it puts you under the constant necessity of writing small letters and cramping the words together. This will diminish its usefulness when it comes to study and review. Moreover, small pages allow little room for indentations, for when you have reached the second or third indentation, you are so far to the right of the page that there is scarcely space enough for legible writing.

4. Number each page, and at the top of each mark the title of the subject, e.g., History, English or Psychology, and, under that, the specific phase of the matter treated.

5. Write fairly large. Small, cramped writing is difficult and annoying to read.

6. Some claim that a pen, in preference to pencil, is an aid both to legibility and to precision.

7. For the sake of brevity cultivate the habit of using abbreviations wherever it is possible. Any unabridged dictionary will furnish you with a list of standard abbreviations. Cultivate the use of them so thoroughly that their use becomes second nature for you. Some of the standard abbreviations which may be employed in ordinary note taking are:

ad inf.	*ad infinitum,* Latin for "to infinity"
ad fin.	*ad finem.* Latin for "at the end"
app.	appendix
bk.	book
cf.	*confer,* Latin for "compare"
chap.	chapter
e contra	Latin for "on the contrary"
e.g.	*exempli gratia,* Latin for "for example"
et seq.	*et sequens,* Latin for "and the following"
etc.	*et cetera,* Latin for "and so forth"

ff.	following
gov.	government
n.b.	*nota bene,* Latin for "note well"
p.	page
philos.	philosophy
ref.	reference
viz.	*videlicet,* Latin for "namely"
seq.	*sequens,* Latin for "the following"
id.	*idem,* Latin for "the same"
i.e.	*id est,* Latin for "that is"
yr.	year
v.	*vide,* Latin for "see"
vs.	*versus,* Latin for "against"
wk.	week

Certain symbols may often stand for entire words or groups of words, for instance:

$=$ may stand for "is" or "are"
$\neq$ may stand for "is not" or "are not"
$>$ may stand for "is greater than"
$<$ may stand for "is less than"
$\therefore$ may stand for "therefore"
& may stand for "and"
? may stand for "doubt or question"

All the days of the week, the months of the year and nearly every branch of study, like geology, mathematics, etc., have abbreviated forms which are commonly recognized. Never spell out a numeral. Always put it down in the form of a figure.

Besides using the standard or commonly recognized abbreviations, invent original abbreviations for yourself. If a certain word occurs repeatedly in a certain lecture begin to abbreviate immediately. Abbreviate it down to a single letter if you please. In a single psychology lesson the word "remember" may occur a hundred times. It is all about remembering. What is the use of writing out such a long word in its entirety every time you need it in your notes? "Rem" or a single "R" may be quite sufficient. Some experienced note takers, when they anticipate a word is to recur repeatedly in the course of a lecture, write it out in full the first time and thereafter refer to it by using only its initial letter, leaving a space of appropriate length to be filled in at leisure when they study their notes. Never write out in full when an abbreviation will do as well.

8. While there is some advantage to writing out the main topics with grammatical completeness, either in the form of a statement or a ques-

tion, the subordinate headings and subheadings need not be written with such completeness.

9. If you are uncertain about the meaning of a specific point, check it with a question mark and attend to its clarification later.

10. If you miss a point entirely, don't bother your nearest neighbor in an attempt to supply it. Just leave a blank space to denote the omission. If the point is important, it will probably be repeated. You may get it when the lecturer recapitulates the matter or from another student at the end of class.

11. Make your notes intellectual performances marked by originality. Set things down in your own words whenever possible. If you honestly disagree with a point as developed in class, record your disagreement. Do not be antagonistic; be humbly honest and alert. If you have difficulty in understanding a point or think you have perceived some contradiction or inconsistency in the matter as treated in class, record this also. There is room for all these collateral notes on the free page to the right, if you are using the "double-entry" system. All this will furnish additional matter and incentive for further study. Remember that when you are making your notes you are honestly bearing down on the matter and not merely copying.

Suggestions

1. Be sure that you know the exact difference between "complete" and "concise"; between "irrelevant" and "repetitious."
2. Examine your last set of notes taken in class and judge its merits from the standpoint of completeness, conciseness and freedom from irrelevant and repetitious matter.
3. Would you prefer a stenographic report of a lecture to a set of notes made out in the form of an orderly outline?
4. Why did you select the kind of notebook which you are using at present? Would another kind be more suitable?
5. Do you see any special advantage in taking notes with a pen?
6. While taking notes in class, what do you do when you miss an important point? What should you do?

CHAPTER XI

Examinations

Examination time is often a dark hour in the life of a student. For many it is a periodic terror. Ordinary activities cease, and amid anxiety and dread, textbooks and notes are poured over in a last frenzied attack to whip the matter into shape and "get by" the examination. Then there is a lull of inactivity till the next examination looms forth to darken a student's life again. Reviewing and preparing for examination is one thing that the college student usually does inefficiently.

COMMON SENSE

In later years you will smile at these examination anxieties. The maturity that comes with retrospection will reveal that most of your anxieties were unfounded and a little childish. It is to your advantage to get a sensibly mature view of examinations while you are still in college and do your smiling now. It will add to your peace of mind and make you a better student.

Strike a sensible attitude toward the whole matter of examinations. Your instructors are generally very considerate and fair and, having been students once themselves, understand the little difficulties and confusion that attend your approach to examinations. They want to see you do well, for it is to their credit as teachers that you do. Examinations are not invented to torture you. They are necessary and beneficial. Would you want to attend a college where no examinations were held and students were never asked to give an account of what they have learned? Understand, then, that periodic examinations, in spite of your unpleasant reactions to them, serve quite useful purposes and that you, the student, are their principal beneficiary.

PURPOSES AND ADVANTAGES OF EXAMINATIONS

In the first place there must be some kind of check on the material learned. You have a right to expect some kind of certificate or assurance of the quality of your collegiate performance. But your instructor cannot give you any kind of rating as a student unless he has a method of sampling your work. A comprehensive, periodic test is the best way to do this. Your daily grades will, of course, assist the instructor to measure the quality of your work, but in classes of ordinary size, every student cannot be given an opportunity to recite daily.

The "A," "B" or "C" which you receive at the conclusion of the examination period is a fair testimonial or certificate of the quality of your work. But you ought to be aware that it is only an approximate rating. There is no such thing as an exact measurement of knowledge and intellectual performance. You can determine the velocity of the wind and the pressure of the atmosphere with absolute exactness down to a fraction. But there is no such minute mathematical exactness in measuring mental achievements. *All grades or notes are to a certain degree inaccurate.* Between an "A" and a "B" student there may be actually little or no difference. A little nervousness during examination, a slight oversight or lapse of memory may change an "A" to "B." A little luck or a happy guess may change a "B" to an "A." No sensible person looks at "A" and "B" grades and takes them as literal readings of intellectual ability. Neither should you.

Moreover, examinations reveal the student to himself. Self-deception is so easy that it is usual. We are all inclined to overrate our own accomplishments. Submitting yourself to an impartial judge is the best way to correct the excesses of self-appraisal. If your grades are consistently low, they need not discourage you, but they should open your eyes to an obvious fact. They do represent a fair but approximate estimate of your scholastic standing. In ninety-eight percent of the cases, if your standing is very low, it may be greatly improved by more study or better study technique. If your standing remains consistently low in spite of the fact that your amount of study is near a sensible maximum and your study technique reaches a point of optimal efficiency, pleasantly recognize your limitations and do not pretend to be a genius. You do not have to be a genius or an exceptionally talented person to be useful and happy.

At any rate examinations are a fine stimulus for good work. Nearly everyone does better under the pressure of necessity. The very necessity that you will be called upon to "render an account of your stewardship" is a potent incentive to perform the stewardship of study well. Look upon your examinations as friendly angels challenging you to better work. Be honest enough to admit that if all examinations were to be called off for one semester, there would be an immediate slump in the amount of serious work. Examinations do make you strive to achieve. And that is why you are in college.

Another advantage is that examinations afford a very favorable opportunity to integrate the course as a whole. If you study for each class as you should, you are making daily additions to your knowledge. But you may be just adding part to part, without ever pausing to review the whole matter as an integer. As I have observed in Chapter VIII, there are valuable advantages in understanding a piece of matter as an integer. New lights and relationships will reveal themselves which could not be clearly understood until the whole matter is completed and reviewed together. A review is valuable at any time, but especially at examination time. For then the matter is more or less definitely completed, giving you your first opportunity for a comprehensive review of the entire subject.

Again, an examination requires a certain amount of intensive and thoughtful writing. Even though you shrink away from such writing, it is a valuable aid to good thinking. Writing makes you think. Whenever you put your pen to paper, you are instantly challenged to think your best.

So put away your peevish complaints about examinations. They are merely necessary, natural disciplines and friendly aids to better work.

The advantages of examinations extend even to the instructors. They reveal to him the general ability and background of his class, thus enabling him to adjust himself to the requirements of the group. The results of an examination may also reveal to the instructor deficiencies in his own teaching methods. No instructor knows just how much of his matter is really "going over" until the results of the first examination are known. With the results of the first examination, it may be evident that he has taken too much for granted, covered too much matter or failed in his method of presentation. A good instructor is always interested in the grades earned by his class. If there are too many failures, it is evident that he has failed as a teacher. Many a professor has humbly examined his conscience after reviewing the general results of an examination and, let us hope, has repented his own mistakes.

PREPARATION

A good preparation for examinations begins with good daily work. Each day's lesson, starting with the first, prepares you for examination. If you add to this frequent reviews covering various sections of the work as they are completed, you ought to be able to pass an ordinary examination without much extra studying. It would be a phenomenon if you fully satisfied the requirements of each day's lesson and flunked, nevertheless, the examination.

But a good final review immediately before the examination is necessary for the best results. It is this final review that often and unnecessarily disturbs and depresses the student. This review will naturally be more intense and comprehensive than former ones, but, provided your daily work has been conscientiously done and you budget your time wisely, there is no reason why it should not be done in a leisurely, efficient manner. After all, it is not a problem now of learning the matter for the first time. The matter, presupposedly, has already been learned and learned thoroughly. It is merely a process of refreshing your memory, perfecting your understanding of certain points and coordinating them into some kind of logical structure. It is simply your final swing at the matter and not a substitute for neglected work.

In making your final review, it is advisable to write up a brief outline of the whole subject, setting down the important topics of the question and arranging them in a natural, logical rhythm. You will then have before you a kind of map of the subject without details. For supplying the details the outlines recorded in your notebook will suffice.

A thorough final review should not be confused with cramming. Cramming is a last-minute drive to learn hastily an extraordinary amount of material and to make it stick long enough to meet the requirements of an impending test. The crammer is trying to learn in haste at the last minute what he should have already learned at leisure. Cramming is an uninteresting, dreary, distressing task. It is also a wasteful expenditure of energy, since matter so learned is usually superficially learned, quickly forgotten and usually leaves the mind in a state of confusion. This is the penalty for neglect. Its only profit is that it may enable you to "get by"— the very lowest of academic achievements. If you find it necessary to cram, do so and take the penalty without complaint.

PREDICTING EXAMINATION QUESTIONS

Try your own hand at predicting your own examination questions. Nearly all students do this in some vague, haphazard fashion. But do it deliberately. Write down fifteen or twenty questions on the subject matter, wording the questions as neatly and scientifically as you can. You are bound to hit a few of the actual examination questions directly, and many of your predictions will be very close to the actual questions. It is quite possible to anticipate practically the whole list of examination questions.

"But is it as easy as all that?" Why should it be so difficult? After all, there are only a limited number of questions that can be asked about any particular subject of moderate length. It is the *matter* which determines the questions, not the fiendish ingenuity of the instructor. Instructors do not sit up late at night figuring out trick questions. They ask only natural questions suggested by the matter itself. What can be difficult about turning the subject material into an interrogation? This is exactly what the instructor does when he makes out the list of examination questions.

"But the questions asked will frequently be determined by what the instructor regards as important or unimportant." Very well. You have a fine opportunity to learn the personal preferences of the instructor by observing him in class. If he stops to emphasize a point and returns to it repeatedly in the course of his lecture or set of lectures, you know it is one point he will probably have in mind when he sets up his final examination questions. Then observe the kind of questions he asks in class, especially in reviews just preceding the examination. Write them down in your notebook. Some of them will surely turn up in his examination. If quizzes are a frequent occurrence in the daily class work, there will scarcely be a single examination question that has not already been asked and answered in class. I am not disclosing too much of the secrets of the teaching craft when I say that it often happens that an instructor will ask a question in class *because* he has already made up his mind to ask it at examination time. As a professor, I have more than once come into the classroom a few days before the examination with the questions in my pocket and nonchalantly asked every one of them of the class before me. No instructor is so secretive and unpredictable that he does not give some clue, consciously or unconsciously, as to the material on the coming examination.

I advise you to anticipate your questions not to coach you in outwitting the examiner, but because of the positive advantages of the method. First, making out a series of pertinent questions on a given subject creates a demand for thought and study. You have to *know* something about the American Revolution, for instance, before you can ask twenty sensible questions about it. Imagine one ignorant of logic trying to ask ten good questions about it. Second, it is stimulating. There is something intellectually invigorating in making a crisp question and trying to answer it with perfect precision. Third, it makes a good rehearsal for the examinations because it makes you feel at home with questions. Some students, even good ones, show a little timidity and fright when suddenly confronted with a question. Somehow or other the bottom seems to drop out. They often say, "I know, but I can't answer satisfactorily." They are not at home with questions or are too slow organizing their knowledge to meet them squarely. It calms you down wonderfully and arouses your self-reliance when you pick up the examination questions and recognize many of them as your own. An examination can, after all, be a pleasant and exhilarating event.

There is an advantage to several students working together to prepare for an examination. Under right conditions collaboration in study is a profitable and stimulating venture. But the right conditions are important. The group should be small, say four or five. Otherwise you have a convention on your hands with all the grotesque inefficiency of such a body. Membership in the group should be selective, i.e., members should be earnest students with about the same general ability. Otherwise equal contribution from several minds, which is the chief advantage of such a collaboration, is not possible. Two or three meetings should be sufficient, and no meeting should be held until each member has had time to review all the matter for himself. Under no circumstances should the collaboration introduce "loafing" or exempt one from serious individual study. When the members meet they may compare their individual summaries of the matter and discuss the lists of predicted examination questions. If specific topics are parceled out to different individuals for more searching study, this should not relieve the other members from reviewing these topics as they would ordinarily do. There should be no loafers or mere auditors. All should study and contribute. It should be a real contact of mind with mind.

DON'T WORRY

Be nonchalant and do not worry. Provided that your daily work has been satisfactorily and conscientiously performed, there is little danger of actually failing, and your final review, though more intense than ordinary, should be a calm and interesting procedure. Yet in spite of this fact, too many students certainly fret and worry too much about impending examinations. Some students are worriers. I still remember from my own college days an earnest student who furnished a lot of amusement by actually worrying about the outcome of examinations during his first week at college, before the rest of us had even thought about them. He was a worrier of unexcelled ability. Never worry about examinations. Never worry about anything. If you have shirked your work to such an extent that you can read the handwriting on the wall and know that you are destined to flunk, there is nothing to do but flunk good naturedly. So work hard and be nonchalant. "If you want to do your best in an examination, fling away the book the day before, say to yourself, 'I won't waste another minute on this miserable thing, and I don't care an iota whether I succeed or not.'"* If you are really good at worrying, try James's advice.

IT DOES HAPPEN

What has been said so far refers to the general preparation for the examination. But good students who are well prepared sometimes turn

---

*William James, *Talks to Teachers on Psychology and to Students on Some of Life's Ideals* (New York: Henry Holt & Co.), p. 223.

in a poor examination paper, and the grade which they receive is definitely below what their general stock of knowledge and mental ability deserve. This does not mean that the instructor has been unfair or too exacting. The examiner has only the paper before him, and it may be a rather poor paper although the writer of it may be a good student. But the examiner must consider the merits of the paper. Sometimes a student returns to the classroom a minute after finishing his examination and says: "Professor, I got the third question all wrong. I don't know what happened to me. I just couldn't think. But I know the matter." And the distressing protestation may be sincere. I have a great deal of sympathy for good students who occasionally hand in a poor examination paper. Many little things may interfere to prevent them from getting the grade to which they are entitled on the basis of knowledge and ability. Nervousness sometimes causes temporary lapses of memory and hinders the processes of concentration. Students may misread or omit a question, or absentmindedly set down the wrong word while thinking of the right one. These things happen to all normal people, and they are sure to happen during an examination when the student is working under unusual stress.

DOING YOUR BEST

Presupposing, then, that you have prepared well, I submit the following suggestions as aids to help you to do your best in the actual work of composing your examination paper:

1. *During the whole period while examinations are in progress keep to your regular routine of sleeping, eating and exercising.* Especially retain the needed hours of daily rest and sleep. Do not study at the expense of sleep. When you are tired and sleepy, go to bed if it is your regular time for retiring. If you are budgeting your time properly, there should be ample time for everything without too much crowding and without any serious encroachment upon needed hours of sleep. Irregularity and loss of sleep are likely to induce a state of nervousness or mental agitation.

2. *Start well.* Plan to arrive for the examination just in time. If you arrive five or ten minutes too early, you are sure to find the classroom a scene of excitement. Students are standing around in little huddles, leaning over books, predicting calamities, etc. If you come too early you cannot insulate yourself from this absolutely worthless flutter of excitement. If you come too late, there will be a measure of excitement and hurry in getting down to work. Come to class just in time to take your seat comfortably and calmly and be ready for the start.

3. *Come to your examination fully equipped.* Bring whatever equipment you need: pencil, paper, eraser, etc. Be sure that your pen has ink. I never knew an examination where someone's pen did not run out. But don't encumber yourself with anything unnecessary. Leave your books and notes at home.

4. *Read over the general instructions carefully.* This is especially important if the examination is the objective type. In nearly every examination there are some students who lower their grades by failing to observe the general directions. Note if there are any "double-credit" questions. If there is an option of answering ten out of twelve questions, remember that the examiner will grade you on the first ten you have answered on your paper, even though you have answered all twelve. There is always a temptation with some students to disregard options and answer all the questions asked—a profitless procedure which merely adds to their labor and expenditure of time, but nothing to their grade.

5. *Read over all the questions before starting to write.* The advantage of this is threefold. It shows you how the questions are related to each other and may prevent overlapping answers. Some examinees, for instance, will get irrelevant matter in one answer which really pertains relevantly to another. Then it gives you the benefit of "overthoughts." "And what are overthoughts?" When thinking hard about a question a stream of thoughts is sometimes evoked in a volume quite beyond what is needed to answer it. We find we have more ideas than we actually need or can use. There is a spillover of ideas which are called "overthoughts." But some of these overthoughts may be just what is needed to answer another related question. Moreover, time spent in carefully reading over the questions is your best time to choose which you will answer, provided there is an option. The earlier you make your choice and get the matter settled the better. With your choice once settled, it is easier to keep your thoughts confined to relevant channels.

6. *Estimate the time.* If you have three hours to answer ten questions, you know that you have on the average of eighteen minutes for each one. When half of the time is up, you ought to be finished with the fifth question. Of course, in gauging your time ample allowance must be made for unexpected difficulties, for rereading and for rechecking your answers and for an occasional pause to rest. Give yourself a sufficient margin. At any point in the examination period, especially during the first half, you should have a fair assurance that you are not taking too much time. If you see that you have plenty of time, don't hurry. The observance of this rule will spare you the inefficiency of a last-minute rush to finish.

7. *Answer the questions in order.* In some examinations, as in philosophy and history, the questions may follow in logical sequence. Answer-

ing one question brings you right up to the point of answering the next one. When you reach question eight, you may discover that its answer has already been suggested by your answer to number seven. You lose the value of this interrelation of questions if you skip around with your answers. Besides, in jumping about you run the risk of misnumbering, which may lead to omitting a question unintentionally. But if you are stalled completely on a question, do not spend a great deal of time drilling your memory; leave a blank and continue with the next question. The right answer may suggest itself in the course of answering the others. The blank space will remind you that a question remains unanswered.

8. *Start writing without a loss of time.* If there is a hesitancy about starting, warm up by writing several sentences on a piece of scratch paper. It is like priming a pump. The way to start is to begin. Momentum and interest grow with application, even though the initial efforts are listless and awkward.

9. *Understand exactly what the question requires.* If there are several parts to the question, like a, b and c, mark your answers similarly and take them in the same order. If the question says "define and illustrate," two things are required, viz., a definition and an accompanying illustration. The two are not the same. If you overlook the illustration or identify "define" and "illustrate," you answer only a part of the question. If you are asked for proof of an assertion, give it and omit any facts or history connected with the assertion which you may happen to know. Make your answer fit the question exactly as a key fits a lock. Hit the nail on the head. An examiner will seldom give you credit for an answer that misses the point, even though it is faultless and correct as far as it goes. Sometimes a student attempts to twist the questions to make it fit the data which he has carefully prepared. I once knew a student who had notoriously neglected his work throughout the course, but when it came to examination time he merely prepared perfect answers to a set of questions which he himself had made out. During the examination period he wrote out his answers just as he had prepared them, completely ignoring the questions asked. To the discredit of the examiner who graded his paper, he received a passing mark. But such substitution, whether intentional or unintentional, is nearly always noted and entirely discounted by the examiner. The material in your answers must not only be correct, it must satisfy the requirements of the question. Careful attention to the specific demands of the question will often spare you the penalty of missing the point.

10. *Make your answers concise.* Conciseness is getting down to the point and expressing it effectively without unnecessary elaborations. This does not mean that your examination paper should be full of epi-

grams. Sometimes the question may require elaboration and full explanation. Conciseness merely means that your paper is not loaded with unnecessary padding, which does not contribute to the development of the thought required.

Some examinees never seem to know when to stop writing. Two or three sentences are strung out, each saying the same thing with tiresome repetition. If one proof is required they are sure to give two. If no proof but only an illustration is required, they are sure to give a proof any way. When they find a topic which they know very well, they are inclined to pour out everything which they have ever learned about the subject. They hit the point, but go to the other extreme of burying it beneath an overload of irrelevant material.

In case of doubt it is much safer, of course, to write too much about a subject than too little. But a paper padded with irrelevant matter labors under several disadvantages. It is certainly a loss of time, for no examiner gives extra credit for material, even though it is correct, which is clearly over and above the requirements of the question. It makes the examiner suspicious of whether the examinee really understands the point or whether he has hit it by accident. In some cases he may even be inclined to discount the ability of the student for his lack of acumen and discrimination. It is rather unkind to the instructor because it requires of him extra work in reading and grading the paper. Grading papers is a laborious and tedious task, and many verbose, padded examination papers may add several unnecessary hours to the job. It shows, moreover, a poor understanding of the real purpose of an examination. When an instructor makes out a list of examination questions, he certainly does not intend to require you to write everything you know about a subject. The questions are merely intended to dip into the matter of the course here and there to get a sample of your knowledge. If these samples are satisfactory, he judges that the rest of your knowledge is also satisfactory and grades you accordingly. You do not have to prove to him that you know more about the matter than the sampling questions demand. That is presupposed.

11. *Use a scratch sheet.* You may employ such a sheet to write down pertinent thoughts that come to you before you are ready to use them. It often happens that in thinking and writing about one question, a valuable idea occurs concerning another question further down in the list. It may be a name, a date, etc., which is likely to escape your memory by the time you are ready for it. Then, there are valuable overthoughts. Write them down, as they come, on a scratch paper if you anticipate any danger in recalling them later. If a question is long and requires logical development, make out a tentative preliminary outline of your answer on your scratch sheet. Such a sheet is also convenient for practicing the

spelling of a word, working out a tentative diagram or drawing or warming up for a question.

12. *Make your paper legible, neat and interesting.* Use ink, in preference to pencil, and write in your best form. An illegible paper written in pencil is a torture to read. You have nothing to gain and everything to lose if the instructor is in a bad humor when he has finished reading your paper. Paragraph your answers suitably and underscore certain words if they are of key importance. This is evidence of order and discrimination. Write out your answers in complete sentences and in the best style of English at your command. But do not be too formal and unnatural. Remember that clarity is the most essential characteristic of good writing. If your sentences are incomplete, ambiguous or hampered by structural complexities, your paper will be a difficult one to grade. You cannot expect the instructor to read your paper several times in order to make out what you mean. If he cannot discern your meaning after the first or second reading, he will likely conclude that you don't know what you mean yourself, and the count is against you. Practice writing with such clarity and simplicity that the meaning of a sentence jumps up and hits the reader in the face. Write as interestingly as possible. Do not be afraid to introduce a little humor here and there provided that it be natural, in good taste and relevant.

The observance of these points produces a favorable psychological effect upon the examiner. Upon picking up an examination paper to grade, the instructor may see at a glance that he is in for a slow torture. His torture may increase as he proceeds. He may be so tortured that he comes to the end of it in a state of impatience or ill-humor. If this is your paper, your miserable writing and composition have added nothing to your account, to say the least. Write so legibly, neatly and interestingly that the very form of your paper speaks in your favor.

13. *If the examination is a long one, pause and relax about every twenty minutes.* Hard mental work makes great demands on the nervous system, and it is not good to keep the bow taut over long and continuous periods. Youthful brows should not be prematurely wrinkled, not even with thought. When physical weariness and brain fog set in, your mental efficiency quickly declines. It is best to rest before fatigue is manifested. It is more sensible to prevent mental or physical fatigue altogether than to relieve it after it has arrived.

14. *Give your paper a thorough rereading at the end of the examination just before you hand it in.* Many students are quite surprised when they receive their papers returned with all the errors and omissions checked. The errors are theirs, to be sure, but they can hardly believe it. Many absurdities, ambiguities, wildly wrong answers, misspelled words

and omissions could be avoided entirely by a few minutes spent in careful rereading. This checkup should be made at the end of the examination period when you are far enough away from the time of the original writing to review it with a little coolness and calm.

Suggestions

1. Enumerate the various advantages and purposes of examinations as discussed in this chapter. Do you agree with the author? Would you omit any of the advantages listed? Would you add any?
2. Would you vote for the elimination of all examinations? Candidly state the reasons for your answer.
3. From your own experience and the reading of this chapter, comment on this statement: "A final general review before examination is necessary not to pass, but only to obtain a higher grade."
4. The only way to convince yourself that predicting examination questions is possible is to try it. When your next examination approaches, try your hand at predicting the questions in advance using the suggestions made in this chapter.

CHAPTER XII

Planning Time

Books have been written on the precious value of time and the sin of squandering it. But college students are often like children in their reckless disregard of the swift march of time and the opportunities which go with it. Once you have grasped the tremendous importance of the fleeting hours and days and have seriously determined to turn them to your profit, you have made a decisive step forward in your profession as a student and perhaps laid the foundation of a future successful career. If you live a life of normal length, the realization of the importance of time and the smooth rapidity of its passage will someday dawn on you in a somewhat startling way. When this realization comes relatively late in life, it is accompanied with a certain melancholy self-reproach for the vast quantities of time that have already been wasted. Time squandered can never be recovered. It is gone, with all its opportunities, beyond recall. The repentant squanderer can only return to the uncertain future lying before him and resolve to make the best of that. The squandered past will always remain an irremediable loss and a sorrow without the conventional silver lining.

ILLUSION

Realize now, once and for all, that time is not an unlimited supply renewing itself from day to day. Many of the world's great men and women in the fields of literature and science had made their immortal achievements and were dead by the age of thirty. But these were only rare exceptions to the general rule. Youth is subtly tempted to dawdle away the years at college with the expectation of getting down to work at some later time. It seems that there will always be plenty of tomorrows. But the time for earnest application is now and not later. If life looks long to you now, and it seems that there will be plenty of time for all your hopes and aspirations to mature—this is an illusion.

An efficient, profitable use of every hour that comes to your disposal is a habit that cannot be learned too early in life. If you are earnest in making the most profitable expenditure of time, deliberately make out a daily schedule which will allot the hours of each day to definite tasks.

I suggest that you make out a tentative or partial schedule which will only include the *absolutely necessary* items of activities and the time expended on each. A sample form will be found on page 114. It is made out, more or less, in the form of a day calendar. Every day of the week has its allotted column. Hours of the day are noted from 7:00 A.M. to 10:00 P.M. Each block represents an hour of time. Naturally, the arrangement into hours is arbitrary. In some cases there may be an advantage to subdividing the hours into half-hours. Remember that this is your schedule and that you are in command.

One student followed my advice and turned in the schedule reproduced on page 114. His week demands 15 hours of class. His 21 meals and toilette call for 17½ hours. He has a part-time job on Saturdays which commands 5 hours, and Sunday worship requires one hour. All taken together the whole week, from rising to retiring, require 38½ hours of time. This is the unavoidable minimum. The student here has deliberately disregarded time for study, recreation, etc., because he intends to allocate these activities to his second and permanent schedule.

As the student now looks over his schedule, he observes at once that he has 66½ hours in every week which are at his disposal and command. These hours are his available time fund. He may squander them recklessly and without profit, or he may wisely invest them to his lasting advantage. Everything will now depend upon how he will invest this weekly endowment of time—his health, his success in college, and perhaps his success in life and his future career.

I returned the skeleton schedule to the student and requested that he fill out the vacant spaces representing the 66½ hours with other normal activities which make up the normal life pattern of a modern student. Study periods, I told him, are more profitable if they immediately follow the class or lecture period while the matter is still hot and fresh. His skeleton schedule indicated that he allows himself nine hours of sleep. Perhaps this is actually more sleep than he needs, but "Sleep" should not be reckoned merely as the hours of actual slumber but the whole time that is incidental to rising and retiring. "Toilette" would include washing, bathing, shaving, etc., but not trips to the beauty parlor or to the barber. These should be bracketed under separate headings. "Classes" might include, besides the actual lecture or laboratory periods, the time spent in transportation or walking to class. If transportation demands considerable time, make a separate item of it. "Reading" includes all types of reading, viz., newspapers, magazines, novels, etc., which cannot be classified as studying. "Work" means not only regular, remunerated labor, but also such minor chores as tidying up the room, shining shoes, pressing clothes, etc. Under "Social" come dances, parties, theater going, concerts, etc. Under "Religious" record not only attendance at divine service, but also meetings of religious societies, Bible reading, and private devotions of any kind. Record nothing under "Athletics" unless you are an actual participant. Time spent as a spectator of a football game should be listed under "Social" or "Recreational." Every day calls for little things to do, odds and ends, which are impossible to classify. Lump them together under "Miscellaneous." Time should also be allotted to "Correspondence" of all kinds.

SKELETON SCHEDULE

	Mon.	Tues.	Wed.	Thurs.	Fri.	Sat.	Sun.
7 A.M.	-------	---- Toilette and Breakfast ---			--------	---------	--------
8							
9	English	Spanish	English	Spanish	English		Divine Service
10	Math	English	Math	Science	Math		
11							
12 P.M.	Lunch	Lunch	Lunch	Lunch	Lunch	Lunch	Lunch
12:15							
1	Science		Science			Work	
2	History			History	History	Work	
3						Work	
4						Work	
5						Work	
6	Dinner	Dinner	Dinner	Dinner	Dinner	Dinner	Dinner
7							
8							
9							
10	Retire	Retire	Retire	Retire	Retire	?Retire?	?Retire?

The student finally returned his permanent schedule to me. It is reproduced on page 116. It deserves consideration and study. You will notice that the plan is not too tight or too narrow. It is not likely to pinch or squeeze. It allows a certain freedom and flexibility, which are necessary. There are free hours in every day of the week. He has one free morning, two free afternoons, and two free evenings. Any part of this free time can be utilized for extras such as theme papers, reading assignments, research requirements, or additional study if required. If necessary, he can easily shift a study period from the time he assigned to it in his schedule to some other free hour. Occasional dates, dances, an evening at the theater, or an unexpected caller will not interfere with his work. The liberal scattering of free time has made his schedule flexible enough to take care of them all. He can retire or rise later than usual without throwing anything out of gear. Sticking to this schedule will be a practical guarantee that he will rank very high in scholarship and class standing and still enjoy all the social and recreational advantages of college life.

MAKING THE SCHEDULE PRACTICAL

In making up a practical schedule, you may find some assistance in the following suggestions:

1. In the amount of time devoted to studying, each subject must be considered in the light of the student's own personal experience. The time needed to study a given subject will depend, of course, upon the subject itself, the intellectual ability of the student and his general preparation and background. There is a generally accepted principle that there should be two hours of study for every hour of classroom treatment. But do not consider yourself bound by an axiom. No one but yourself can determine the amount of time you should allow for studying a given subject. No two students will make out identical schedules.

2. A period of study should strike a mean between extreme length and extreme brevity. It takes time, as a rule, to get warmed up to a subject. A period of study that is very brief is often a very inefficient expenditure of time. On the other hand, if the study period is extremely long, fatigue and gradual lack of interest retard efficiency.

3. Ordinarily one may study just as efficiently during the day as during the evening hours. Students who are constantly saying, "I can't do any serious study till evening," may only be deceiving themselves or have gotten into a psychological rut. If you postpone all your serious work till the evening hours, what are you doing with the free hours of daylight? Generally, less eyestrain occurs when studying in daylight,

PERMANENT SCHEDULE

	Mon.	Tues.	Wed.	Thurs.	Fri.	Sat.	Sun.
7 A.M.	-------	---- Toilette and Breakfast ---			--------	Miscella-neous	
8							
9	English	Spanish	English	Spanish	English	Cor.	Divine Service
10	Math	English	Math	Science	Math	Cor.	Reading
11	Study Math	Study Math	Study Math	Study Math	Study Math		
12 P.M.	Lunch	Lunch	Lunch	Lunch	Lunch	Lunch	Lunch
12:15		Shopping					
1	Science	Cor.	Science	Study History	Study Math	Work	
2	History	Reading	Study Science	History	History	Work	
3	Study Science		Study Spanish	Study Math	Study Math	Work	
4	Study Spanish	Recreation		Study	Study	Work	
5				History	History	Work	
6	Dinner	Dinner	Dinner	Dinner	Dinner	Dinner	Dinner
7	Study Spanish	Study Science	Study Science	Study	Study	Social	Social
8	Study	Study	Study Science	English	English		
9	English	English	Study Spanish	Reading	Recreation		
10	Retire	Retire	Retire	Retire	Retire	?Retire?	?Retire?

which may be a very important factor for some students. Sternly discipline yourself to study efficiently any time the opportunity occurs—morning, afternoon or evening.

4. There is an advantage to studying a given subject as soon as possible after its classroom treatment while the details of the lecture are fresh and clear in the mind. This is especially true if you find the subject difficult to master. A long gap between class time and study time almost certainly reduces personal interest and ease of comprehension. In some cases a long lapse of time is almost disastrous.

5. The order in which certain subjects are studied is important. If certain subjects are somewhat similar, separate their respective periods of study. For instance, do not study mathematics and philosophy immediately one after the other, or French immediately after Latin. A round of mathematics is better followed by a subject quite unrelated to it, e.g., history.

6. Some subjects are more efficiently learned by two or three separate study periods rather than one prolonged attempt. This principle is true especially of subjects which are intrinsically difficult, like mathematics and philosophy, or with subjects demanding considerable memory work, like foreign languages. If philosophy is extremely difficult for you, take a vigorous swing at it, say for an hour, and then stop. Then take it up as vigorously later that day or the next. With each attempt some light will dawn. At the end you may experience a sunrise.

7. In long periods of study, viz., three or four hours in the evening, plan for a few brief pauses to relax completely. These intervals may be devoted to resting or to some recreational diversion, such as reading a newspaper, listening to the radio or watching TV.

8. Start special assignments, like theme writing, term papers, book reviews, etc., at the earliest possible moment. The free hours on your schedule may be temporarily assigned to such extra work. This is thrifty foresight which will eliminate frenzied, last-hour efforts which too often disturb the calm and order of a student's life. Getting down to an extra assignment early will improve the general character and originality of the finished product by giving your own thoughts on the subject time to mature and by supplying many relevant ideas derived from your general reading. You thereby give these new ideas time to mature and come to the surface when you need them.

9. Don't expect your day to proceed exactly as planned by your schedule. There will always be some sudden or unexpected interruptions. Learn now to expect the unexpected. If you are suddenly interrupted, say by the arrival of an unexpected visitor, calmly lay your schedule aside and forget it. Time that is lost may easily be compensated for later. Remember that your schedule is only a friendly guide to help you and not a straightjacket. You are the master of your schedule and not its slave.

10. Your schedule may require subsequent readjustment and repair. Having followed it for a while, it may be evident that certain study periods may be shortened; that others should be lengthened; that certain study periods should exchange places; that daytime study is more practical and profitable than evening study; that one evening is better left free than another. Practical experience will almost invariably reveal certain defects in the schedule which ought to be corrected.

11. When your schedule has been finally adjusted to the point of maximum practicality, stick to it. Don't be a fool and go back to your old, slipshod, don't-know-what-comes-next method of study.

ADVANTAGES OF A SCHEDULE

Some students are reluctant about making out a time budget because they suspect that it will be boring and tiresome to be restricted to such a methodical mode of life—an objection which is very strange coming from those who need methodical restrictions the most and who have never tried them. If you are suspicious of self-imposed regularity of studying, at least give it a trial.

The advantages of such a planned schedule will gradually reveal themselves to anyone who seriously makes the test. Among its advantages is that it fosters development of character, for it makes constant demands for punctuality, order and judicious investment of time. It keeps the student conscious of the ideal of his profession—scholarship—and subordinates everything else to it. It substitutes ease, leisure and security for haste, anxiety and nervous rush. It may be valued most by the ordinary student because it eliminates the dreadful necessity of last-minute cramming. Cramming is never a pleasure to a student, but he often submits to it merely as a matter of sheer necessity. Nearly always its necessity is the result of sloth or a lack of foresight. Working according to a practical schedule will be a cure for both. A student guided by a sensible plan experiences a sense of power because he is in command of himself and the master of his time.

Suggestions

1. Have you ever seriously considered how the amount of time which you expend in studying and profitable reading compares with the amount of time consumed in recreation, amusement, light reading and loafing? Would finding out help you?
2. Would you loaf less if you knew exactly how much time you spend loafing?

3. Observe yourself for one week and make out an exact record of how you are spending your time at present. Then study the record thoroughly. Are there any significant surprises? Does such a record make you feel satisfied with the way you are spending your time? Does it suggest any methods of improving your personal efficiency?
4. Do you know any person who does an extraordinary amount of work and still seems to have sufficient leisure? How do you explain this? Ask the person himself how he does it.
5. Think over the following statements:
   a. Forethought saves time.
   b. Making out a plan is merely a practical exercise of forethought.
6. Read a good book on the "value of time."

CHAPTER XIII

Mastering Words

The number of words in the English language has been estimated as high as 800,000. But *Webster's New International Dictionary* (1961) lists over 600,000 word entries. So for practical purposes we may suppose that 600,000 words are the ceiling.

LANGUAGE CHANGES

However, a living language changes constantly. It changes in two ways. The first way is by accretion or a growth in the number of words. Every year new words are coined and added to the original stock. On the other hand, there are thousands of words now in practical use that will one day be discarded and become obsolete. Nevertheless, obsolete words remain a part of the language and must be retained in our dictionaries because they must be understood in order to read the literature of past generations. The Bible is a good example of a book widely read but still containing thousands of obsolete words. Our dictionaries, which grow larger and larger with every new edition, plainly prove that the frontiers of a living language never stand still but are always advancing.

A living language also changes internally, i.e., by alteration in the meaning of words. From time to time words change their meanings or take on additional new meanings with use. In fact, there are very few words which we use day after day which do not change in meaning from one generation to the next. There are several instances of words in the English language which have actually reversed their meanings in the course of time—a very interesting phenomenon for the student of words.

Our language, then, is a seething throng of words constantly growing in volume and shifting their meanings, and nothing can arrest its changeable character. No one can know all the words of the English language or keep abreast of its constant changes. Although there will never be a ceiling to your vocabulary, you can set out deliberately to enlarge and improve it. The work of developing a vocabulary is the progressive task of a lifetime. One's vocabulary is always in a state of continuous alteration, a work that is never finished. But it can be moved forward indefinitely, nearer and nearer to the actual ceiling. Your years of high school and college are a period especially suited to a large, healthy growth in the number of words under your command. For your future vocabulary these years are springtime. If these years pass without adding abundantly to your stock of words, your vocabulary will probably remain stunted and lean for the rest of your life.

PASSIVE AND ACTIVE VOCABULARY

Your passive or comprehensive vocabulary is the body of words which you understand when you hear or see them on the printed page. It may be called your reading vocabulary. Your active vocabulary is the body of words which you actually use, either in writing or speaking. You understand many more words than you actually employ in either writing or speaking. And you employ many more words in writing than in speaking. You may even know many words which you deliberately refrain from using. It is estimated that one's passive vocabulary is three to four times greater than one's active vocabulary.

HINDRANCE OF A LEAN VOCABULARY

A lean vocabulary is a constant hindrance to a student. It retards the speed of reading, as we have observed in Chapter VI. It pinches you when you attempt to write and cramps you when you attempt to speak, especially when you attempt to speak in public.

It also tends to limit your range of reading. It is true that there is a surprising amount of noble, serious literature which may be quite intelligently read without straining even a very ordinary vocabulary. Even though your stock of words is small, the door to good literature is not absolutely sealed, nor is a man with a slight vocabulary necessarily a shallow thinker, any more than a man with a rich vocabulary is necessarily a deep thinker. Still it is true that a very limited knowledge of words is a definite obstruction to reading and to that extent a hindrance to serious study and thought. Words are tools of thought, and we do our best, other things being equal, with the best tools.

It is not difficult to understand how a lean vocabulary chokes good reading. Readers with only a slight command of words, even though they are inclined to serious thought, are easily allured to literary tripe since this kind of writing is so prevalent, so easy to obtain and so well adapted to their limited range of words. They are estranged from dozens of subjects and alienated from hundreds of books because they cannot read them with any degree of ease. If they do take up subjects and books beyond the depth of their vocabulary, such reading will always take on the proportions of a heroic feat and will most likely turn out to be an uninteresting and disagreeable performance.

Do you want to derive the maximum delight and profit from reading, to write effectively and to speak with unhampered ease? Then get yourself a wide, sure command of words. This should be one of your definite aims. Your four years at college are the most propitious period of your whole life for the development of a rich and varied vocabulary. It is an opportunity which will probably never be repeated.

TESTING YOUR VOCABULARY

The extent of the ordinary man's vocabulary is much larger than is commonly supposed. S. Stephenson Smith opines that the average reading vocabulary may be near 9,000 words,* and that a person of high school education or its equivalent may have a range of from 9,000 to 14,000 words. (Cf. Smith, p. 13.) Your vocabulary has already been started, but there is practically no limit to its further refinement and growth.

It is extremely difficult to determine even approximately the range of your active vocabulary. But there are several methods of testing the extent of your passive vocabulary. There is one test which you can easily try out for yourself. It consists in sampling the dictionary for words at one hundred regular intervals throughout the entire volume. Use any standard unabridged dictionary. Note the number of pages devoted to definitions. There may be, for instance, 2,373 such pages. In this case, you begin your test on page twenty-three and continue to sample every twenty-third page thereafter. A hundred such samples will carry you through the entire dictionary at regularly spaced intervals. On page twenty-three take the first word in bold type at the top of the first column to the left of the page. If you know this word, you have one point in your favor. Leaf forward to page forty-six and test yourself on the word that appears there at the top of the left column. Thus you continue sampling a word from every twenty-third page. On a separate record sheet keep your score, i.e., record exactly the number of words you know and the number you do not know. Your record sheet may indicate that you have recognized fifteen out of the hundred sampled words. This means that you know approximately fifteen percent of the words con-

---

*S. Stephenson Smith, *The Command of Words* (New York: Thomas Y. Crowell Co.), p. 1.

tained in that dictionary. The next step is to discover how many words the dictionary actually contains. The preface of the dictionary will usually supply this information. If it does not, you will have to compute the number for yourself. This is done by determining the average number of words to a page and multiplying this figure by the total number of pages. The final number thus obtained will give you the approximate number of words which are listed in the entire dictionary. Suppose you discover that the dictionary contains about 400,000 words. Multiplying this number by fifteen percent, you arrive at the final result of 60,000. You know at least 60,000 words. In making this test do not demand of yourself a precise dictionary definition. If the word tested has several meanings, the point is in your favor if you know any one of its meanings well enough to use it correctly in a sentence. Of course, as stated earlier, in making the test only a standard unabridged dictionary should be used.

This is an interesting test to make and is a fairly accurate estimate of your reading ability. You might preserve your score and make the same test, altering the position of the word on the page, a year later. Contrasting the two scores will reveal to you how much your vocabulary has grown during the interval.

METHODS OF DEVELOPING A VOCABULARY

Everyone's vocabulary is always on the increase. Our first words came to us from hearing others speak. As you pass from grade to grade, your store of words slowly increases. In high school the increase is somewhat accelerated, and the process continues at a fairly rapid rate throughout your college career. Thereafter, the rate of increase may slow down. But new arrivals keep coming in through business contacts, travel, general reading, etc. Whether you realize it or not, the frontiers of your vocabulary are always creeping forward. The increase may be sluggish, desultory or sporadic. But there is never a very long period of time when your vocabulary comes to an absolute standstill.

There is no danger, then, that your vocabulary will cease to grow. But there is a danger that it might grow too slowly. No one can ever say that his vocabulary is perfect or good enough. There is never an absolute limit to the number of words which you might profitably command. The serious student of words, not satisfied with the ordinary sluggish increase which comes inevitably with daily experience, will deliberately employ methods to increase his vocabulary. These deliberate methods are not new. They have been employed by everyone who has achieved any notable command of words. Some of them may seem tedious and laborious to a novice. But they become quite interesting with use. A fine mastery of words is not an accident. It is the result of conscientious work.

All of the following suggestions for improving your vocabulary are valuable. But some are more valuable than others.

READING

The first method is extensive and varied reading. Reading makes your vocabulary march. Without it it limps. Merely reading, without the benefit of a dictionary, is a prolific source of new words. Of course, without the aid of a dictionary many words will escape understanding altogether. But there are hundreds of words which can be learned satisfactorily from the mere context, i.e., their reference to what precedes and what follows. The general pattern of thought in which a new word occurs is often quite sufficient to reveal its meaning. The meaning of thousands of words, like "nonchalant," "brash," "armistice," etc., have been revealed and admitted into our vocabulary by merely meeting them in their proper context. Even such unusual words as "hauteur," "insouciant," "sangfroid" and "macaronic" may pop with surprise when they are found tightly and neatly tucked into their proper context.

For best results reading must be both *extensive* and *varied*. The two terms are not synonymous. You may read extensively, but not variedly, and vice versa. If you confine reading to novels, you may be reading only extensively. If you read much, but in many different fields—novels, history, philosophy, botany—your reading is both extensive and varied.

USING THE DICTIONARY

For best results reading should be supplemented by the constant use of a dictionary. Every student should own a good desk dictionary and be adept at using it. Words whose meaning cannot be clearly recognized from their contexts must be diligently looked up. The proper use of a dictionary requires a familiarity with its system of abbreviation and the significance of diacritical marks. A good dictionary tells you more than the meaning, pronunciation and spelling of the word. In many instances it supplies you with the derivation and history of the word. It also tells you of the linguistic status of the word, i.e., whether it is archaic, colloquial, provincial, dialect or slang. You must know the actual status of the word before you can command its use in writing and speaking. Looking up the word "besom" you are informed that it is an archaic or poetical term. It is, therefore, not a matter-of-fact word which can be suitably used for general purposes. With this detailed knowledge of the word you can handle it with refinement and restraint—the signs of a master.

When you hunt down a word in a dictionary, note also its various meanings. Words with multiple meanings are very common in every language. Some of the simplest words in our language can be employed in a dozen or more senses. "Graft" has fourteen meanings; "change" has thirty-eight; "post" has forty and "stock" has forty-three. You never really appreciate the richness of language until you have explored the wide variety of meanings often attached to the most common word. Complete control of a word's usage requires a comprehensive knowledge of its various meanings. Nowhere does a master of words display his skill to better advantage than in the adroit use of common words. For instance, "tool" used as a *noun* is a very common word. But do you know this word well enough to use it as a *verb?* In its verb form it is a rare word.

A reader often shirks the task of hunting a word in the dictionary because of the labor involved and the annoyance of interrupting his reading. If a strange word is of such importance that it dominates the whole passage, it should be looked up then and there in spite of the attendant labor and annoyance. Otherwise the sense of the passage is killed. Ordinarily, however, the strange words we meet are not of such commanding importance. In this case the unknown or doubtful words may be checked at the margin of the page as they occur, or they may be listed on the flyleaf of the book, together with the page references to the text where they appeared. Then they are looked up together at one session with the dictionary. Thus words are added to your vocabulary, batches at a time.

WORD LISTS

A more methodical and effective method is keeping a word list. Get a supply of convenient-sized cards, say 3 by 5. Whenever you meet a new word, write it down on the card. If you are reading a book, the card may be conveniently used as a bookmark. When the card is filled, look up the words and set down the meanings after each word as briefly as possible. Study the words over for a few minutes to be sure that you have learned them, and file the card for future study. Within several weeks you will have a very interesting set of words, all taken from your own reading.

Study these cards from time to time. It is an excellent way to capture odd moments which would otherwise be wasted. This is merely the application of the principle of overlearning. (Cf. Chapter VIII.) Of twenty words looked up today, ten may be forgotten tomorrow. How often have you looked wistfully at a word and said to yourself, "I have seen you before and have looked you up, but I don't know what you mean"? There is no better way of rescuing hard-learned matter from sinking through the meshes of automatic forgetting than by reviewing and overlearning. The meanings of words must be learned and nailed down. Word lists will help you nail them down.

Several word fans can get together and compare their word lists. It is an interesting game, and each person profits by the reading and labor of the others.

Another advantage of keeping word lists is that it enables you to gauge very accurately the number of new words that are added to your vocabulary within a given space of time. When you are once aware of the astonishing number of new words which you can bring into the fold of your vocabulary, say within a year's time, you will be stimulated by a sense of achievement.

SYNONYMS AND ANTONYMS

The study of synonyms is a valuable aid not so much in extending your knowledge to new words, as in refining your appreciation of the shades of meaning which belong to associated words already in your vocabulary. A good master of words is selective in his use of them. When he has an important idea to convey, there arises in his mind a cluster of related words, and out of the cluster he extracts only those which express the idea with maximum precision. The idea is expressed without smothering its sense in a smoke cloud of words. There is brevity, exactness and finality to his style. But to secure good selectivity in the use of words there must be good selectivity in your understanding of words. Words must lie in the mind in bundles, and the separate words in each bundle must be weighed with refinement and judiciously distinguished from their comrades.

The deliberate study of synonyms is the best way to achieve a refined knowledge of words. Words must be studied not only in isolated states, as they are found in the dictionary, but according to families or related groups. They must be studied in bundles. For this particular kind of study *Roget's Thesaurus*, Crabb's *English Synonyms*, Putnam's *Word Book* or Fernald's *English Synonyms, Antonyms and Prepositions* will render valuable service.

The study of antonyms is also important. It is often necessary in writing or speaking to pass from one thought to its opposite. Besides, certain words are better clinched in the memory if they are immediately referred to their opposites. For instance, to remember the meaning of "sangfroid," contrast it at once with "agitation" and "nervousness."

PUTTING NEW WORDS TO USE

Transfer new words from your passive to your active vocabulary as soon as possible. You are not the complete master of a word until you can summon it for use in either writing or speaking. Here the college student has an exceptional advantage over the ordinary reader. For the daily requirement of recitations, theme writing, term papers, etc., offer frequent opportunities to put into use the new words acquired in reading. You must actually use a word a few times before you feel at home with it. After a word has been turned to service, it soon snuggles down and becomes a familiar servant in your household of words.

Letter writing, a literary art which has lost ground in recent years, also offers a suitable opportunity for limbering up your vocabulary and mustering words into actual service. Writing in a diary is another simple method of fertilizing an active vocabulary. In everyone's passive vocabulary there are thousands of words and phrases hovering about ready to be captured and sent to work. Any kind of serious writing or speaking will help to transfer them to your active vocabulary.

But I do not believe that you ought to design to employ immediately every new word encountered in reading. Pedantry is a serious mistake. A good vocabulary is merely a good reserve of words which will respond to the call for service when and if you need them. There should never be any ostentation in the use of words, never an attempt to startle or impress others. As a rule, the more simply a thing is said the better. If you sink the sense of the written or spoken word in learned verbiage, you are a pedant, not an artist. In a public address, especially, you must select words which will tell upon the audience. Some words should be rarely used in public speaking. For instance, you should know how to handle the term "precisian," but it is peculiarly unsuitable as a spoken word because of its phonetic identification with "precision." In commanding the service of words, you must know when to muster them in and when to muster them out.

Still, the rule holds good that you should endeavor to employ new words in speaking and writing as soon after learning them as possible and always with discrimination and within the limits of modesty and good taste.

ETYMOLOGY

In looking up the meaning of a word in the dictionary get as much of the etymology of the term as possible. Knowing the etymology of a word means knowing its source, its origin or how it came to enter our language. In every unabridged dictionary a brief description of the term's etymology is given between brackets just before its definition. In using a dictionary do not disregard the valuable information contained between the brackets.

No serious student of words can afford to neglect the study of etymology. Colleges cannot lay out a set course in every subject. Etymology is one of those subjects which a student must teach himself. Both profit and surprise await anyone who will take the time for serious etymological research. Every word in the English language has a birthday. It has an ancestry, was born in a certain manner, came into use at a certain time and has probably gone through a process of change. Sometimes a word gets into use by mere accident, like "atlas." Sometimes it is deliberately invented, like "automobile." Sometimes it owes its origin to a mistake, like "gypsy." Sometimes a word is midwifed by the name of an individual, like "dunce," philippic" and "mausoleum." Whenever the circumstances surrounding its birth are recognized, the word itself becomes an object of interest. The history of nations, man's errors, his degradation and his aspirations are all recorded, to a certain degree, in the words of his language. Words are like fossils, which if known and properly interpreted are historical revelations of the race.

The source from which a word is derived ordinarily determines its fundamental meaning. No matter how many various extensions and figurative applications the word has acquired in its descent through generations of use, all of these will be usually linked to and controlled by its primary signification. Thus, the etymology of a word, even though it does not correspond exactly with the modern use of the word, will always shed light upon its current meaning. A word etymologically understood takes on a flavor and aroma which can hardly be appreciated by one who is ignorant of its etymology. Knowing, for instance, that the English word "novelty" is derived from the Latin word "novus" which means "new," you are in a position to grip the trunk meaning of the term. It implies something which is new, fresh or unseen before. "Novelty" will no longer be taken as the equivalent of "trinket," for a trinket may be an ancient heirloom. You will never say, "The *novelty* of the experience thrilled him," when you mean that he was thrilled by the "uniqueness" or "weirdness" of the experience. Similarly, the true meaning of "inveterate" is clearly understood when you interpret the term as a direct derivative from the Latin "inveteratus," which means "long standing." An "inveterate habit" is merely one which has been "long standing" or "long established" and not necessarily one which is "firmly established," although there is a connection between a habit's long establishment and its firmness. In the light of their etymology, "inveterate" and "confirmed" will stand out in their true relationship.

Following is a sample list of common words whose understanding will be clarified to a degree of refinement by knowing their derivations:

angel	circumlocution
anonymous	exaggerate
astonishment	gospel
atonement	horrify
cadaverous	impecunious
cathedral	innate
chiropractor	manipulate

marine	sculpture
mortal	scruple
philosophy	subterranean
prejudice	supercilious
radical	unique
rupture	urbanity
salient	

If you really know these words etymologically, you begin to manipulate them with a new handle. You will understand why they came into the English language and why they came to mean what they do. An etymologist gets a little merriment out of realizing how two words, "prestidigitator" and "chiropractor," for instance, are applied to different professions and skills, although they have practically the same root meaning.

There is another class of words which are in no sense translations or interpretations of the original words upon which they are constructed. In this class of words there seems to be a mysterious gap between the meaning of the word and the parent word which produced it. For instance, we have the curious word "canard." It means a false and extravagant story invented to mislead. Yet "canard" comes directly into the English language from the French word "canard" which means "duck." A Frenchman would be surprised to know that his word for duck has been adopted into English to mean a "false story." There is no natural relationship in meaning between the French mother word and its English daughter. Still there is a reason why the Frenchman's word for duck has come to be the Englishman's word for a lying exaggeration. There are thousands of such strange adoptions of foreign words into the English language. Most of them can be explained. The study of the history of words reveals how many of our common words are the spawn of mythology, geography, popular errors and superstition, and the incidents and accidents of history. To this class of words born of curious incidental lineage belong the following:

academy	lazarette
atlas	lunacy
balbriggan	malapropism
boycott	mausoleum
calico	mercurial
candidate	muslin
dunce	paraffin
epicure	philippic
gerrymander	rhubarb
gypsy	tantalize

An ordinary dictionary cannot be expected to give a full history of a word. In this field of etymological lore the *Oxford Dictionary*, Matthew's *Use and Abuse of Words* and Trench's *Study of Words* are the best sources of study.

CLASSICAL ROOT WORDS

Familiarize yourself with the more common classical roots or root words which enter into the construction of thousands of English words. This is only a modification of the etymological approach to new words. The student of Latin and Greek has an unquestioned advantage here, for these two languages supply us with about sixty percent of our words. But any ordinary student with little or no knowledge of Latin and Greek can learn to recognize and interpret a hundred classical key words which are woven and interlaced into the fabric of the English language. These key words occur and recur in modified forms especially in scientific and philosophic nomenclature, and always with the same primary signification. Once learned they are a handle to thousands of words.

S. Stephenson Smith, in his book, *The Command of Words,*[*] gives a list of ten Latin words which, together with the two Greek words *"logos"* and *"graphein,"* form the basis of 2,500 English words. The ten Latin words are:

facio	—do or make	*pono*	—place
duco	—lead	*teneo*	—hold or have
tendo	—stretch	*fero*	—bear
plico	—fold	*mitto*	—send
specio	—see or observe	*capio*	—take or seize

The Greek word *"logos"* meaning "word, reason, thought or science," has sired no less than 156 English words.[†] Some of the more common derivatives are archeology, biology, catalogue, decalogue, dialogue, epistemology, etymology, logic, monologue, phraseology, physiology, prologue, tautology, theology, travelogue.

The Greek word *"graphein,"* which means "to write," is nearly as fertile as *"logos,"* making its English appearance in the form of "graph." From this one Greek word we get: addressograph, autograph, biograph, dictograph, geography, graphic, lithograph, monograph, multigraph, paragraph, photograph, seismograph, stenographer, telegraph and typography. The meaning of every one of these words involves the basic idea of "writing."

---

[*]Smith, p. 67.
[†]Ibid.

Even a knowledge of the more common Latin and Greek prefixes will help to identify the meaning of many terms and to establish them in the memory. In the following lists you have the principal classical prefixes, together with their meanings and sample words which they help to form. A careful study of these prefixes, and attention to their repeated occurrence throughout your reading, will indicate how many of our common words descend from Latin and Greek ancestors.

Latin prefixes:
>   *ab*—from—abduct, abscond
>   *ad*—to, next to—adhere, adjacent
>   *ante*—before—antedate, antecedent
>   *bi, bis*—twice—biannual, bifocal
>   *circum*—about, around—circumlocution, circumnavigate
>   *cum**—with, together—coexist, collaborate, compliant, commensurate
>   *de*—away from—dement, detract, deduct
>   *duo*—two—duplex, duet, duel
>   *ex*—out of, from—excommunicate, extricate
>   *in*—in, into, on—insinuate, implant
>   *inter*—among, between—intermural, intermingle, interweave, intervene
>   *intro*—within, inward—introspective, introvert
>   *male*—badly—malevolent, maltreat, malhandle
>   *post*—after—postpone, postmortem
>   *pre*—before—prearrange, premonition
>   *pro*—in place of, in favor of, forward, before—pronoun, proslavery, proceed, prologue
>   *sub*—under, below—submarine, subterranean, subject
>   *super*—over, above—superhuman, supercilious
>   *trans*—across, beyond—transgress, transmit
>   *tri* (from *tres*)—three—trinity, trident, tridimensional
>   *ultra*—beyond—ultraconscious, ultramodern
>   *vice*—in place of—vice-president, vice-chairman

Greek prefixes:
>   *amphi*—on both sides—amphibian, amphitheater
>   *an (a)*—not—anomaly, amorphous
>   *anti*†—against—antislavery, antifreeze

---

*Changed for euphony to *co, col* or *com.*

†This Greek prefix occurs in more than 480 English words. It should not be confused with *ante.*

di (dis)—twice, twofold, double—diploma, diplomat
dia (di)—through, across, asunder—diagnose, diagonal
ec (ex)—from, out of—eccentric, ecstasy
epi (ep)—upon, on the outside, among—epidermis, epidemic
hyper—over, in access of—hyperbole, hypercritical
hypo—under, beneath—hypodermis, hypocrite
meta—beyond, after, change, in reverse—metaphysics, metaphor,
    metamorphism
mono—alone, one—monologue, monogram, monograph
para—beside—paragraph, parasite
peri—around—peristyle, periphery, periwig
poly—many—polysyllable, polygamy
proto—first—prototype, protomartyr
pseudo—false—pseudonym, pseudograph

THE GOAL

A good command of words means that you have a rich stock of words to draw from, that you can use them with precision and that the right word will respond to the need of the moment. In other words, the goal is a vocabulary of good size, together with facility and precision in its use. Enough has been said to indicate that such a mastery of language is not acquired by any brief and simple process. It is the cumulative result of many years of study, experience and patient search. But you should know now whether you are moving in the direction of the goal. If you are, you can be satisfied that further study and experience will bring your vocabulary nearer and nearer to the ideal of perfection.

Plan now to enlarge, enrich and refine your vocabulary by deliberate, methodical means. But remember that your aim is to be the master of words and not their slave. Words should always remain servants of thought and not the master of the thinker. Their function is simply to express thought and not to serve one's vanity by making others wilt with admiration. To strain one's vocabulary for big, strange words when small, simple ones will do just as well is mere pedantry, an ignoble trait in anyone, but a vice in a scholar.

Suggestions

1. Read any volume of O. Henry and note the striking way in which he employs words which are unfamiliar to you. How do you think O. Henry succeeded in building up such a huge vocabulary? Consult his biography.

2. Read a play by Shakespeare, carefully noting his effective use of small words.
3. Does a wide knowledge of words guarantee a ready use of words? Does the ability to coin expressions, combine words and create telling figures of speech depend more on imagination and thought than upon an extensive knowledge of words?
4. Why do people use slang? Why do we sometimes prefer slang? What should be your attitude toward the use of slang?
5. Draw up a definite, practical plan for increasing your vocabulary.
6. Have you ever spent a continuous hour studying the dictionary?
7. Make out a list of words which have come into the English language with the invention and use of the automobile. Make out another list of new words which have appeared in the language since you started high school; since the beginning of World War II. Considerable time and thought will be needed to make out such lists.
8. Read a book or a good treatise on the subject of etymology, philology or the history of the English language. Trench's *Study of Words* is a classic. Other suitable works are: Greenough, *Words and Their Ways in English Speech;* White, *Words and Their Uses;* Matthews, *Essays on English* and Smith, *The Command of Words.*

CHAPTER XIV

Using the Library

The character of college libraries has greatly changed within recent years. As late as the middle of the last century, and in some cases later, many colleges had no libraries at all. Until a rather recent date some colleges restricted the use of their libraries to a few hours of certain days of the week. These were called "library days." On all other days the doors of the library were locked. Today the library is conveniently and prominently located on the college campus and is open to the students practically all hours of the day and night seven days a week.

Today the modern library, with its opportunities of reading, studying and research, is one of the outstanding educational achievements of the age. An inexperienced student may be amazed when he first learns of the vast range of material which a modern library puts at his immediate disposal. By learning to use its facilities he commands the printed word. Not only does it place the materials of research within his reach, but it offers him a suitable place for reading and studying. The library is not merely a place to get books; it is a place where studying and actual research work are done.

KNOW YOUR LIBRARY

Entering college, one of the first things you should do is to acquaint yourself with the library, with its arrangement, content and the general facilities which it affords for your particular field. In the same way you should familiarize yourself with whatever other libraries there may be in your local community. This general knowledge of library facilities will save you a great deal of time later when you will actually need them.

Some colleges offer freshmen a course of two or three lectures designed to interest them in the college library, to acquaint them with its opportunities and to teach them how to get about and actually use it. If no such lectures are given in your college, make an inspection tour of the library yourself. Spend several hours or more at it. Note its general layout, the "stock" rooms, reading rooms, reference shelves, newspaper and magazine racks, the location of books and materials related to your course. Library shelves may be "open" or "closed." When a patron is allowed to step up to the stacks and remove a book himself, the shelves are spoken of as "open." Some libraries, however, do not permit this freedom but have a special library assistant who is appointed to remove the book from the shelf for the patron. In this case the shelves are spoken of as "closed." Usually in large libraries the shelves are closed to prevent the danger of books being misplaced by careless patrons. If the book "stacks" are open, sample a few of the books that you are likely to need, but be sure to return them to the exact positions from which they were drawn. The books are arranged in order and a misplaced book is temporarily lost. Get a general idea of how the books are classified and arranged on the shelves. If you desire information and direction, ask the librarian or one of the librarian's assistants. You should know the rules of the library and the proper way of withdrawing books. Whatever the rules are, obey them conscientiously. They are necessary for the orderly distribution of books and are made only in the interests of the patrons themselves. Ignoring the rules of the library shows a selfish disregard of the convenience and rights of other readers.

Your hour of introduction should give you a fair idea of the general content of the whole library. This is important, for it will indicate what you may expect from the library and how far it is able to satisfy your particular needs.

Getting an idea of the general content of a large library may seem to the uninitiated a hopeless task. A sense of bewilderment sometimes overcomes one standing in the midst of thousands of books! Books in such vast numbers seem to frustrate their purpose. Yet it is possible within three or four hours to get a fair idea of just what a library contains. With this knowledge once acquired, you are in command of the situation and quickly lose your sense of bewilderment. The library then takes on a friendly air and is soon regarded as a convenient and necessary adjunct to your profession as a student.

To master the general contents of a library and to test its value for your purpose, familiarize yourself with the following:

1. the card catalogue
2. magazine indexes
3. dictionaries
4. word books supplementary to dictionaries
5. encyclopedias
6. almanacs
7. various reference books on special subjects

CARD CATALOGUE

Every library has a "card catalogue." It is an index to the entire library. It serves the same purpose as an index to a book. You need not read through a book to know what general topics it treats. Glancing over the index reveals this in a few minutes, and even if the book treats a thousand subjects the index indicates just where in the book the treatment of each subject can be found. So the card catalogue indicates just what books are contained in the library and where each is located on the shelves.

But it differs from a "book" index. In a card catalogue the index reference for each book is contained on a separate card, usually 12.5 cm. by 7.5 cm. These cards are filed in alphabetical order in long drawers set in a steel cabinet. Each drawer is labeled from A to Z, like an encyclopedia.

Somewhere in these files, any given book is usually represented by several different cards. For there are title, author and subject cards. In other words, any book may be listed in three different ways: according to the title, the author and the subject matter. If you want to know whether the library contains the novel *Moondyne Joe* by John Boyle O'Reilly, you may look through the index cards under "M" until you come to *Moondyne,* just as though you were running down a word in a dictionary. If the library contains the book, the card representing it will be there in its alphabetical place. Or you may have forgotten the title of the book, remembering only that John Boyle O'Reilly has written an interesting novel which you want to read. You will then look through the cards under "O." Author cards always list the surname first. If the library contains O'Reilly's novel, the author card will be titled "O'Reilly, John Boyle," and on a line beneath the title of the novel will be given. Or sometimes you may simply want to know what material the library contains on a given subject, regardless of book titles or authors. For instance, you want to know what books the library contains on the subject of bees. The card so marked will furnish a list of books, together with their respective authors, which treat this particular subject. At the end of the list, you may find cross references, directing you to look under "Insects" and "Entomology." Additional material will be found by searching under these titles. Subject cards are of great value for research. One need not lose much time discovering what and how much material the library offers concerning a given subject. Moreover, searching the files under a certain subject title is one of the most efficient methods of making out a suitable bibliography. Studying the card catalogue soon puts you in command of all the books in the library.

To the left of the index card is a number, like 371.3, which indicates the exact location of the book on the shelves. If you want to draw this book from the library, the usual way is to sign a "call slip," a supply of which is usually found somewhere near the file cabinet. On the call slip there are spaces to fill in with the call number, title of book and author, although the call number alone is sufficient. The call slip is then presented at the circulation desk, where it is given to a library assistant who locates the book and draws it from the stacks. In smaller libraries with open shelves you may take the book from the stack yourself. But it is always required, of course, to present the book at the circulation desk before taking it from the library.

MAGAZINE INDEXES

In estimating the general content of a library, special attention should be paid to the magazine indexes. It would certainly be a naive, mistaken notion to suppose that all the worthwhile literature and the valuable information needed by a student are to be found in books. A great deal of valuable contemporary literature makes its introduction into print through the medium of the better magazines. Some of the best of our contemporary writers are frequent magazine contributors. It would certainly be an unscholarly attitude to deny the value of the enormous literary output of contemporary writers whose thoughts come to us through periodicals of the better type. Such material furnishes valuable collateral reading for almost every course taken at college and is sometimes the only source of information on matters of current discussion so often needed for debates, speeches and theme writing. The vast, almost unlimited wealth of valuable magazine material may at first drive the inexperienced researcher to despair. But magazine indexes come to your rescue and afford you an easy grip on the huge output of data and general information furnished by hundreds of contemporary writers. The purpose of these indexes is to guide you directly to the magazines which will furnish you information on the particular subject in which you are interested.

Poole's Index to Periodical Literature is a guide to magazine material issued, in some cases, as early as 1802. The references are to magazines of both American and British publication. Of course, not all magazines are listed. At the beginning of each volume you will find a list of the magazines which the volume indexes. The material is listed by subject only. If you are interested in the question of unemployment, you may turn to the "U" pages and find the word "Unemployment" just as you would find it in a dictionary. After the word "Unemployment" there will be given the full title of the article, the author and the magazine which contains the article together with the issue number and page where it is to be found.

The Readers' Guide to Periodical Literature is similar. It lists magazines issued since 1900 to the present day, with monthly supplements to keep it strictly up-to-date. It does not cover as many magazines as *Poole's Index,* but it has the advantage of listing the articles under author and title as well as under subject.

Besides these general indexes, there are others especially adapted to guide you to magazine material on specialized topics. For example, there are special magazine indexes relating exclusively to book reviews, agriculture, engineering, industrial arts, etc.

After you have consulted the mazagine index, you know what magazine contains the material you want. Your next step is to find out whether the library contains the magazine. You find this out by referring now to the card catalogue. Magazines are bound in convenient volumes. If the library contains bound volumes of *Atlantic Monthly,* for instance, you will find a card in the general catalogue labeled with the name of this magazine. This card will show you at once what volumes of *Atlantic Monthly* the library contains, designating them by volume and number. Some libraries have a separate catalogue for indexing magazines only.

Spend a little time examining a standard magazine index in order to familiarize yourself with its content and makeup and to train yourself in the practical use of it.

DICTIONARIES

The most useful and most frequently used of all general reference books is the dictionary. A good unabridged dictionary is a mine of useful information. It is at least one whose authority is seldom contradicted. Besides giving the spelling, pronunciation, derivation and meaning of words, it furnishes information about proper names and noted names in fiction, explanations of foreign phrases, lists of synonyms and standard abbreviations. At the end of the volume may be found a biographical dictionary and a gazetteer of geographical information. No student can really appreciate the full value of a dictionary unless he has carefully reviewed its contents to see the extensive field of information it actually covers. It is much more than a book giving the meaning of words.

There are many dictionaries of the English language, each excelling in some particular point. A good library may have several standard unabridged dictionaries.

Webster's New International Dictionary is the best known. Its recent revision (1961) is the work of several hundred learned collaborators and lists and defines between its two covers more than 60,000 words,

"the largest number ever included in a dictionary of any language."*
It covers words used in the English language since 1500.

Funk and Wagnall's New Standard Dictionary is less extensive in
scope, limiting itself to "live words" only. It has the special merit of
listing antonyms as well as synonyms, besides offering the reformed
spelling of words.

The New Dictionary of Historical Principles, ordinarily called the
Oxford Dictionary, or *Murray's Dictionary,* is now complete in ten stu-
pendous volumes in adition to a recent supplement. It is a monument of
philological erudition and the most unique and exhaustive word study
which has ever been attempted. The fact that the first volume was
issued in 1888 while the second one was not off the press till 1928 indicates the vast amount of time and labor consumed in preparing this
work. It not only gives the meaning of words, as an ordinary dictionary,
but traces the historical development of the meaning and spelling of
every word used in the English language since 1150. It tells you when
any given word first appeared in the language, the meaning it had at
the time of its initial appearance and how this meaning has changed
through the course of centuries. It is an indispensable source book for
etymological research. Ordinarily, however, an undergraduate student
will have only occasional need for consulting its learned pages.

The Century Dictionary and Cyclopedia is a monumental work of
twelve volumes. It does not minutely treat the development of each
word, as the *Oxford Dictionary.* But it furnishes, in addition to the ordinary definition, much historical and technical data about the thing
defined. It specifically aims to supply concise technical information
about things and processes pertaining to any particular science, art,
trade or profession. It is almost lavish with pictorial illustrations. For
instance, under the term "lace," you will find over three columns of
explanation describing how various kinds of lace are made, together
with two full pages of illustrations. It is definitely more than a dictionary.
As the name suggests, it is a dictionary and encyclopedia combined.

WORD BOOKS

In the study and mastery of words there are many other basic reference books which supplement the work of dictionaries. These are
rhyming dictionaries and studies of synonyms. The study of synonyms
and antonyms is important for the mastery and skill in selecting words
with attention to their precise shades of meaning. The most important
synonym books are: Crabb's *English Synonyms, Roget's Thesaurus of*

Webster's New International Dictionary, 1961 Edition, preface.

English Words and Phrases; Fernald's *English Synonyms, Antonyms and Prepositions* and March's *Thesaurus Dictionary of the English Language.* Crabb's *English Synonyms* is a most useful book for the ordinary student. It carefully explains the fine, delicate shades of meaning of closely associated words which are often used interchangeably. The explanations are further clarified by selected quotations. For instance, it is useful to know the finer distinctions of meaning between the words "happiness," "joy," "delight," and "bliss." These words are not identical in meaning. Knowing when to select one and reject the other requires more than an ordinary dictionary knowledge of the terms. *Roget's Thesaurus* gives an exhaustive group of related words, without explaining their minute distinctions in meaning. For instance, under the single term "length" over a hundred related words are listed. A study of such a work is useful for a speaker or writer seeking amplitude and variety of expression.

ENCYCLOPEDIAS

Encyclopedias rank next in importance as general reference books. They contain information over a wide range of subjects, biographical, historical, philosophical and religious. For easily accessible supplementary reading for almost any branch of study, encyclopedias are unexcelled. You should know what encyclopedias your library contains. They vary a great deal in point of view, style, arrangement and extent of material treated.

1. *The Encyclopaedia Britannica* is now published in its fourteenth edition with twenty-four volumes. Its articles are long and exhaustive in treatment, British in background and point of view and accompanied by illustrations and by useful bibliographies. The last volume contains a detailed index to subjects of lesser importance which are not separately listed among the alphabetical list of articles appearing in the body of the work.

2. *The New International Encyclopedia* is complete in its second edition (1927) with twenty-five volumes. In 1930 a supplement of two volumes was added. *The International Year Book,* issued annually, keeps the encyclopedia up-to-date on current matter. Its articles are shorter than those of the *Britannica,* American in viewpoint and unsigned. In the front part of each volume is a list of contributing authors.

3. *The Encyclopedia Americana,* as revised in 1932, is now issued in thirty volumes. *The Americana Annual* keeps the encyclopedia up-to-date from year to year. It is particularly valuable to students of American

history and government. Its treatment of the World War covers 450 pages. It is the most up-to-date of all encyclopedias of similar scope, although there has been some criticism of its accuracy.

4. *The Catholic Encyclopedia* is issued in seventeen volumes including the supplement and a separate index volume. It is now undergoing revision. Expert and reliable scholars from all parts of the world have collaborated in producing this international work of reference. It is the only work of its kind covering the history, practices, liturgy, doctrines and discipline of the Catholic Church. It is a unique, scholarly compendium containing hundreds of subjects scarcely mentioned in other encyclopedias. For the student of church history, medieval institutions and biographical material connected therewith it is almost an indispensable aid. The index volume contains "courses of reading" which list important general topics for research, like education, history and philosophy, arranged in alphabetical order. Under each topic appears a list of the various articles pertaining to it which may be found in the encyclopedia. The articles are signed and further identifying information concerning the contributors is given in the front part of each volume. Throughout the work there are cross references and numerous bibliographies. It is regrettable that a great many of its learned treatises are uninterestingly written, difficult to read and out of reach of the ordinary reader, a fault which may be partly due to the fact that so many of the articles are translations from foreign languages.

5. *The Jewish Encyclopedia* is a comprehensive, succinct treatment of practically every subject touching upon the history, traditions, customs, literature, rites, theology and philosophy of the Jewish people, past and present. It also contains considerable biographical data of all the important representatives of the Jewish race. Many of the articles are supplemented by valuable illustrations and maps. Since so many modern questions and problems involve the history and traditions of the Jewish race, this unique, scholarly compilation from Jewish sources should not be slighted by the research student.

ALMANACS

Inspecting the general contents of the library, you should note what almanacs it places at your disposal. Every serious student during his course at college should get to appreciate the value of an almanac and familiarize himself with at least one of them. Almanacs are published in one volume, issued annually and report information on a wide scope of material in the form of summaries and statistical tables. It is neccessary to familiarize yourself with the general arrangement and content of a good almanac before you can appreciate the amazing mass and variety of data which it places at your disposal.

Among the most serviceable almanacs are the following: the *World Almanac*, American in its viewpoint; the *New Hazell Annual and Almanac*, British in viewpoint; the *Chicago Daily News Almanac*, very similar in range to the *World Almanac*, and the *Statesman's Year Book*, especially valuable for live material on politics and government.

REFERENCE BOOKS ON SPECIAL SUBJECTS

Besides these broad works of general reference in the dictionary and encyclopedia class, there are many other valuable reference books limited to special fields of research in which the ordinary college student is likely to engage. Your tour of the library should reveal which of these special reference books are upon its shelves.

1. In the field of biography *Lippincott's Biographical Dictionary* is most extensive in its range. It furnishes brief accounts of famous men from the ancient times through to the present day. It also supplies data concerning many biblical and mythological names. *The Appleton Encyclopedia of American Biography* includes names important in American history and life. *Who's Who* is a famous biographical dictionary which has been issued annually in London since the year 1849. Its biographical sketches are restricted almost exclusively to Englishmen and only to those now living. Even the mailing addresses of the listed persons are included. *Who's Who in America,* issued biennially, records biographical data of living citizens of the United States.

2. In the field of geography there are many gazetteers and atlases. A gazetteer is a geographical dictionary, briefly describing and locating rivers, lakes, towns, etc., and listing them in alphabetical order. An atlas is a book of maps. Effective studying and certain types of writing often require consultation of such geographical references. Among the reference books in this field are: *Lippincott's New Gazetteer, Rand McNally's Commercial Atlas of America, Rand McNally's Commercial Atlas of Foreign Countries,* and *Hammond's New World Loose Leaf Atlas.* The latter is a looseleaf volume which allows for the insertion of new maps as these are required.

3. In the field of history there are such reference books as: Larnerd's *History of Ready Reference* in twelve volumes, *Cambridge Modern History* in thirteen volumes, *Ploetz's Manual of Universal History,* a compendium of the history of the world up to and including the World

War, and *Harper's Dictionary of Classical Literature and Antiquity,* including material pertaining to both history and mythology.

If you are interested in history you should notice what books and pamphlets the library has pertaining to the local history of the community in which you live. Local historical societies often issue annual or quarterly bulletins which contain an abundance of important and interesting material omitted from historical books of a more general character. For example, the Ohio Archaeological and Historical Society for many years has published its researches in annual volumes which now total over thirty.

4. In the field of philosophy, look for Baldwin's *Dictionary of Philosophy and Psychology,* consisting of four separate volumes; Mercier's *Manual of Scholastic Philosophy,* published in two volumes; Bakewell's *Source Book in Ancient Philosophy;* DeWulf's *History of Mediaeval Philosophy in two volumes;* and the English translation of the *Summa* of Thomas Aquinas, a monumental work of twenty-two volumes.

5. In the field of literature good reference books are of extreme importance. You should know where to turn to clarify allusions to mythology and fable, and how to run down proverbs and familiar quotations to their sources. For this special purpose there are Brewer's *Dictionary of Phrase and Fable; Bartlett's Familiar Quotations;* Allibone's *Prose Quotations from Socrates to Macaulay* and his *Poetical Quotations from Chaucer to Tennyson.*

Among the most recent of special reference books in literature are: the *Cambridge History of English Literature* in fifteen volumes (1933); and the *Cambridge History of American Literature* in three volumes (1933).

You should know that there is a *Book Review Digest,* published since 1905, which contains summarized reviews and criticisms of the more important books published from year to year; and a *United States Catalogue of Books,* now issued monthly, listing under both title and author all the books published in the United States. This latter index also gives the particular subject treated, the name of the publisher and the price of the book.

6. In the field of public documents, the *Census of the United States* is a monumental volume of statistics published by the Census Bureau. The same bureau also publishes two abridged forms of the census: the *Abstract of the Census* and the *Statistical Atlas.*

In this chapter I have only noted those books of reference which may be valuable from time to time to the ordinary student. But there are other valuable books of special reference in practically every field of research. For instance, there are special reference books in the fields of painting, music, architecture, sociology, political economy, education, engineering, agriculture, etc. There are Bible atlases and indexes to poetry, drama and short stories.

WHERE DO THEY GET IT?

If you are interested or become interested in any of these fields, it is to your advantage to know what data is at your disposal and where it can be found. No matter what the type and direction of your intellectual interests, the modern library is an inestimable help. Many times you may have marveled at the wealth of detailed information and significant data which flows with such ease and in such volume from writers, public lecturers and radio speakers. They seem to abound with telling erudition about so many subjects which seem closed to the ordinary person. There is nothing mysterious or superhuman about such versatility, although it often puzzles the uninitiated. These writers and speakers simply know how to tap the waiting sources of knowledge and put them at their command. One can obtain detailed and accurate information practically about any topic if he knows just where to find it. A good library is an inexhaustible mine of general knowledge and a workshop for the student, lecturer and public speaker. It lays at your disposal the resources of the printed word, which has been accumulating for centuries. Know what your library contains and how to command its resources.

CAUTION

You should use the sources of information, however, with caution. Not all reference works are of equal dependability. You should note the date of the copyright, the character of the author, the association interested in its publication and whether the volume you are reading has been revised or has a supplement. Some books, even standard works of reference, are written and compiled with a bias. This is particularly true in the fields of history and literature. The particular purpose of a book, or its peculiar prejudice, if it has any, may often be detected by reading the introduction or the preface. Sometimes the *publisher* of a book is an indication of its dependability. Some publishing companies are known as producers of worthwhile material. Others, to the contrary, are known as prone to publish books of questionable value or authority. No written word is a guarantee of its own reliability. Its reliability is not enhanced by merely appearing in a book. There must always be due caution in accepting the word of another, whether it be spoken or written.

Suggestions

1. Spend an hour studying the *Oxford Dictionary*.
2. If you should desire technical, concise information about etching, photography or the structure of a camera, what dictionary would you consult?
3. Devote an hour or two comparing Crabb's *English Synonyms* and Fernald's *English Synonyms, Antonyms and Prepositions*. Determine which is better suited to your own needs.
4. Equip yourself with a good dictionary, a book of synonyms, an atlas and an almanac.
5. Read over some article, perhaps on slavery or the Revolutionary War, in several encyclopedias and note the variations of treatment, the differences of viewpoint.
6. Familiarize yourself with the local or municipal library.
7. What other things besides books and reference works does your college or local library furnish? Some libraries have valuable files of prints of art paintings, public documents, newspaper clippings on various subjects, back numbers of local newspapers, etc.
8. If there is a museum in your vicinity, there is probably a small library attached to it which is worth investigating.

CHAPTER XV

Physical and Mental Health

It would be possible to draw up a long list of men and women who have spent useful and happy lives or who have blessed the world with fine literary and artistic achievements while laboring heroically under serious handicaps of poor health. Nevertheless, one's best work is usually accomplished under conditions of sound physical and mental health. Any serious impairment of health, sometimes even a slight impairment, is detrimental both to the quantity and quality of a student's work. Good health, then, must be reckoned among the factors contributing to satisfactory intellectual work.

PHYSICAL HEALTH

Good physical health is the result of heredity, environment and habits. You start out with what heredity bequeathes to you. This is further modified by environment and the habits which you form. You have nothing to do with the initial health fund which heredity gives you. But you can alter and dominate your environment to a large extent, and the formation of healthful habits is practically a matter of your own making. So your health, given a fairly good heredity, is largely, though not entirely, in your own hands.

The ordinary laws of physical hygiene are few in number and all of them quite simple. They deal principally with food, exercise, rest, fresh air and cleanliness. You are presumed to know them by this time.

But a mere knowledge of hygiene will not keep you well. The important thing is to live by them habitually. There is a tendency in a healthy youth to disregard the ordinary rules of health because their repeated infractions bring no noticeable, immediate inconvenience. If he can go for a week averaging three or four hours of sleep each day, he is inclined to imagine that he is a kind of superman and boast of his foolishness as a feat of endurance. But this is a delusion of inexperience and ignorance. No person is a charmed exception to the simple rules of health. If the persistent disregard of them is not followed by any immediate disability, it only means that youth is drawing upon its initial reserve of physical strength. This initial reserve may be abundant, but it is his *only* reserve, and when it is depleted it can never be restored to its original level. This physical reserve is there to meet emergencies and to last through the years of a normally long life. If it is too early spent, there will be little left to meet unavoidable emergencies, and serious trouble may appear in middle life. Nature may delay her penalties but she always exacts them.

Even the most careless person gets serious at times and lives sensibly for brief intermittent periods. But these sporadic periods of sensible living are not sufficient. Living the simple rules of hygiene should be brought to the point where they are followed consistently and naturally day after day and without thinking about them. In other words, their observance should be brought to the point of a smooth-flowing habit.

HYGIENE AND ETHICS

Everyone admits that the observance of the ordinary rules of health is, at least, good sense. But few consider it in the light of a moral obligation, which it actually is. Life is not a picnic. It is a gift of God and given to us for a purpose. In order to live we must work. Our work, whatever it is—studying, working in an office or repairing automobiles— is our duty. In fact, our work and all the responsibilities connected with it make up the major portion of all the duties of life. When a man is at work, he is in line of duty. If the work be neglected or carelessly done, he deserves moral censure. But ordinarily the efficient performance of work requires a certain degree of health and strength. A loss of health or its grave impairment usually causes a serious interference with the regular chores and responsibilities of life. You cannot fulfill your moral obligation of studying when you are sick. If a man suffers an impairment of health because of a wild disregard of the simple rules of hygiene, nothing less can be said than that his consequent incapacitation is self-inflicted. Such a one has culpably unfitted himself for duty and contributed to his own delinquency. His neglect of health is not a matter of innocent imprudence. It is, like lying and stealing, a criminal thing and deserves moral reproach.

The ethical aspect of sensible hygienic living may also be understood from the fact that good physical health has an important influence in the development of one's spiritual life. Physical health has a connection not only with sanity, as nearly everyone knows, but also with sanctity. When one is in healthy condition, it is easier to pray, easier to meet temptations, easier to control your temper and easier to be kind and cheerful. Poor health may occasion many temptations and in some cases renders virtue a most difficult achievement. Health, then, is not merely something which is conducive to longevity and the enjoyment of life. It may actually be conducive to virtue. It has something to do with the proper development of your spiritual life. So its prudent conservation is a moral issue and a matter of conscience.

TWO SUGGESTIONS

Since you are presumed to know the ordinary rules of health, they need not be reviewed here in detail. But two suggestions may be made here which have special application to students.

The first is that any defect in teeth, vision or hearing should receive prompt attention. These defects not only directly affect the work of a student, but, if neglected, may cause serious trouble in later life. It is a good plan to have a physical examination during the vacation period, especially for teeth and eyes, so that any discovered defects may be attended to without interruption of schoolwork. During the course of every school year, much valuable time is lost by students interrupting their work for trips to dentists and physicians. Such interruptions are always inconvenient and costly, and many of them can be avoided by arranging for needed dental and medical attention during the vacation period.

The second suggestion is that a student should take a sensible attitude toward the necessity of physical exercise. Exercise, in proper amount and quality, is necessary for good health. But strenuous exercise, in the form of hard, competitive games, is not necessary. It may be harmful. *No one needs strenuous exercise.* You don't have to be tough in order to be healthy. Sporadic, strenuous exercise is worse than none. The only kind of exercising that really promotes health and longevity is the kind that is moderate and consistent. *Consistency of mild exercise is more important than vigorous seasonal exertion.* You are wise to cultivate some form of moderate daily exercise that will not terminate when college days are over. Make the daily exercise a habit now. It will be more difficult to acquire such a habit in later life, when it will be needed the most.

MENTAL HEALTH

Good mental health is as important for achievement and human happiness as good physical health and is almost altogether of our own making. The vast majority of students who come to college are mentally healthy. Mental ailments of various sorts, which blight the happiness of so many thousands of people, do not ordinarily appear before early middle age. But nearly all of them are preventable, especially if they are recognized in their incipient stages. In nearly every case they grow out of certain mental attitudes and habits which begin to operate many years before the malady actually becomes a serious handicap. Many college students begin to adopt attitudes toward their work and life in general which may be innocent and innocuous enough, but which gradually mature into serious mental ailments in later years. It is of utmost importance for your future success and happiness to get correct attitudes and a wholesome view of life now. You never learn healthy mental traits too early.

The following suggestions may not seem significant to you now, but when viewed through the perspective of years and riper experience, they will be judged to be of critical importance. Many a student pursues his course at college more or less successfully, judged according to scholastic standards, but is laying down mental attitudes which are almost certain to destine him to a life of unhappiness and suffering. Don't let unwholesome mental traits become inveterate. They grow strong and stubborn with age. The longer they stand the harder they are to correct.

PLAY

Learn to play. Don't make each day an uninterrupted application to serious work. Be earnest about your work, but interrupt it frequently by play. The purpose of play is to relax the mind, to change the mental scenery. A child should play much and work a little. An adult should work much and play a little, but he must play. As we grow older, the character of the games we play changes, but we should continue to play. It frequently happens that the games of childhood are broken off too abruptly without any adequate substitution, and we have an adult who is so serious and grave that he has lost both the desire and knack for playing. Such a one disposes himself to mental disorders, at least of minor seriousness. The more serious and exacting your work is, the more need there is for the relish of healthful play. Some pleasure and enjoyment in life are absolutely necessary for a normal mentality.

It does not make much difference what form of play you engage in. Any kind of recreation, suited to your age and state of health, will do. If the form of recreation takes you into the open fresh air, so much the better.

My advice to college students is to devote at least one full evening each week to recreation, play or entertainment. Besides this, one whole day out of every two weeks can be profitably devoted to play. To some this may seem a large order, but I presuppose that you are doing hard, serious work. Make a definite place on your schedule for recreation and play. If you keep it within the limits of moderation, do not imagine that time so spent is lost. It is a valuable investment.

I am aware that college activities usually afford sufficient opportunity for recreation. But the important thing is to continue your play in the more critical and trying days after your college course has terminated. Don't become an overserious, playless adult.

HOBBIES

Cultivate an interesting hobby. A hobby is any side occupation, interest or skill which one finds interesting and to which he may frequently turn as a pleasurable relief from his routine work. It should be something quite apart from your ordinary line of work, pleasing and interesting and of such a nature that it may be carried on at intermittent intervals just as it suits you. It may be a mechanical skill, an intellectual interest or some form of occupation requiring manual labor. It makes no difference, so long as it is something that absorbs your interest and occupies your spare time: collecting stamps, pictures, butterflies or old photographs, painting, music, needlework, cabinet making, gardening, studying trees, flowers, geology, architecture or local history. Almost anything may turn out to be a matter of absorbing interest providing enjoyable relief from your work, once you get into it. It is almost a form of illiteracy to ridicule a collector. To make a collection of mounted butterflies, for instance, is quite an intelligent occupation. It presupposes a certain knowledge of the subject and invites the collector into the extensive field of entomology, one of the most interesting of scientific studies. The collector of stamps has more than his stamp book reveals to the outsider. He has a knowledge of printing, engraving and history which is quite beyond the scope of the ordinary person. You may take it for granted that anyone who has pursued a hobby is, to that extent, a more skilled or learned person than you are. The world teems with interesting things to do and to learn. If there is nothing in the world to interest you, you are like a blind man walking through a garden of beautiful flowers. Perhaps I should say you are like a man who shuts his eyes while a parade is marching by.

A hobby renders an important service. It affords a pleasant relief from the prosaic round of duties which at times becomes wearisome for almost everyone. It also usefully fills up the hours and days of unemployment which are likely to breed ennui and a disgust for life. It makes you an interesting person, promotes contentment and preserves mental health.

Most adults do not feel the need for a hobby until middle life, when mental poise is usually put to the test. But it is difficult to initiate a valuable mental habit just when one needs it. Good habits and wholesome interests do not spring into existence suddenly when they are summoned to meet a need. They should be there before the need actually occurs. As a college student, cultivate some interesting hobby which is quite removed from your scholastic requirements and continue it beyond your college days. Learn to be an interesting and interested amateur in something.

WORK

Work hard. Attack the work which lies in the line of duty with earnestness and vigor. If you have time to spare, make work for yourself. Create projects for yourself, and apply yourself to their accomplishment as earnestly as if they were required. Idleness is a mental hazard. The man who has time to kill is in a dangerous spot.

SERENITY

Cultivate serenity and poise. Anger, irritability and excitement over trifles and unavoidable obstacles keep some people in an almost perpetual mental agitation. The demands of modern life with its speed, rapid-fire radio announcers, jazz music and the insidious intrusion of inflamed, sensational advertisements, keep many people in a constant state of gentle turmoil. Many who call themselves go-getters are merely unconscious victims of mild hysteria. It is really an unhealthy state of excitement, easily mistaken by its victims for an energetic disposition which hinders sound reflection and may lead to unwholesome attitudes, grave in their possibility of destroying happiness.

To foster a spirit of serenity, it is necessary to eliminate, as far as possible, the influences which are antagonistic to it. For example, don't speed where there is no necessity for it, shut off the radio programs of jittery music and meet the inspired, modern advertising appeals with good humor and gentle skepticism.

If you find yourself hurrying excitedly about, ask yourself if there is any need of it and how much time you are actually saving by hurrying. If there is no need to hurry, don't. If there is reason to hurry, resolve to give yourself more time for similar tasks in the future. There can be no justification at all for a state of constant hurry. If you see that you are going to be late for class, do not flutter in excited haste, even though your fluttering would bring you there on time. Just accept the fact of your lateness good-naturedly.

Every day we encounter unexpected delays and disappointments which set our cherished plans at naught. School yourself to meet these daily upsets with complacent calm. Learn to expect the unexpected and feel at home with little emergencies which call for modifying or completely rehabilitating your prearranged plans. If your plane is thirty minutes late, do not wear your nerves down with savage resentment against the company. Take a walk around the airport. You may find the place interesting and you may need the exercise.

Beware of sudden gusts of either elation or dejection. If you simply must gush and gust about a little, get it over with as soon as possible and return to normal equilibrium. Don't mistake excitement for pleasure. Hold yourself more or less to an even track. Any deviation to the right or the left should be justified by the circumstances, and the normal, even tenor resumed naturally, smoothly and as quickly as possible.

Such an attitude of mental serenity makes life more peaceful, pleasant and happy, creates an atmosphere conducive to solid, serious achievement and contributes to length of life. To some who are emotionally rocked about at the mercy of every shifting circumstance of life, this may seem to be an impossible state of mind. But far from being impossible, it is the normal state of mind which you ought to cultivate. Begin by taking the more trivial, daily setbacks and disappointments with resolute equanimity. You may gradually acquire mental poise in meeting all the crises and emergencies of life. And never mind if now and then a mental jitterbug calls you a stoic. Proudly admit that you are one.

WORRY

Worry is the opposite of mental serenity. It is a panicky nervousness, a state of more or less emotional uneasiness accompanied by fear over the anticipated outcome of some present or impending peril.

There are plenty of perils in life, large and small. But worrying about them is nothing more than a bad mental habit. There is nothing mysterious about this habit, except that it seems to grow in spite of its utter uselessness. Like all habits its growth is slow, gradual and, as a rule, an unconscious process. And like all other habits it grows by frequent repetitions until it becomes a kind of psychological mannerism. One does not become a worrier overnight. A good worrier becomes so by constant practice. He begins by worrying innocently over one or two serious things and gradually develops the knack of worrying about nearly everything. He begins by worrying part of the time until he gets so proficient that he can worry about something or other nearly all the time. A good worrier can worry over trifles, but an expert can worry over things that are imaginary or ludicrously remote. It is principally a matter of practice. Hence, there are many degrees of proficiency—some worriers are really better than others—but any degree of the worrying habit is bad, useless and detrimental to health and happiness.

As a rule, college students have not had sufficient time and experience to become professional worriers. But some of them are amateurs off to a fair start. Some of the best worriers in middle life are those who began to practice in college without realizing that they were building up a serious mental handicap which would eventually overshadow their future success and happiness. Student worriers usually do their practicing on such themes as examinations and the welfare of the folks at home.

Professional worriers are usually stubborn. They are not prone to admit that they worry at all. Or if they admit the fact, they rise to its defense by assuming that they worry because they are interested, earnest, thoughtful people. Sensible persons see through the sham at once. For one may be earnest about a thing without worrying about it. Worrying is a sign of nothing but a very bad mental habit.

These remarks may seem defiant and outrageous to a good, determined worrier. For deep in his heart he imagines that his worrying is a sign of superiority, i.e., that it indicates interest, understanding, feeling and sympathy. He is likely, in defense of himself, to imagine that a person must be unnatural and callous not to worry. He has a sly way of assuming that worrying is a necessity and a religious duty. Suppose that there is a student at college who has a brother at home very sick with typhoid fever. He realizes that the outcome may be fatal. He would willingly interrupt his studies to go home if his presence there would be of any real service. But he is not needed at home, and there is nothing that he could do to help the situation. Being deeply interested in the case, he appreciates receiving reports from time to time of his brother's condition, but he does not expect hourly health bulletins and long-distance calls from home. So he just remains at school and continues his normal, customary work. To a worrier this would seem to be a callous attitude. But why is it callous? Why is it virtuous to interrupt a useful work for something useless? It is, in reality, a sensible attitude and quite consistent with the requirements of Christian charity. It is the professional worrier who is self-centered and leaves nothing to the Providence of God while mistaking his mental alarm for charity and sympathy. So the habit of worrying can be explained, but it can never be justified.

When a perplexing situation or an emergency turns up, the outcome of which may affect you adversely, try to grasp it intelligently and do what you prudently can to prosper the outcome. But when you have done that, let that be the end, absolutely the end, of the matter as far as you are concerned. There is nothing to do but continue your work. Mulling over a bad situation in a kind of fever of alarm and despondency is a stupid, unprofitable performance. Whatever time and energy are thus spent are lost—absolutely lost. Worry is mental friction—merely an indication of a waste of good thought.

If you are inclined to worry, think over the following:

First, worrying is bad mental manners. If you don't adopt an attitude of sensible nonchalance about things you cannot help, you are preparing yourself for much needless suffering in this life, without contributing a single thing to the lot of the human race. It is all loss and no gain.

Second, a great deal of feverish anxiety, for instance about the results of examinations, is often an indication of exaggerated selfishness. Your main interest lies probably in your ego. If the worst comes to the worst, what of it? If it seems that you are going to flunk, completely reconcile yourself to the event before it happens. It might even be an interesting event. Even a flunk is not an irretrievable disaster. It might even be a wholesome experience. The chagrin of flunking is entirely in your own mind.

Third, worrying never changes the results for the better. It is an absolutely sterile mental occupation. If your uneasy fears prosper the situation, by all means, worry. But since they do not, all your worrying is lost mental motion.

Fourth, even an amateur worrier should know that most of the things he has worried about in the past have failed to measure up to his best fears. Practically all the expected catastrophes that caused worrying never happened. The worrier has a past record for inaccuracy that is ludicrous. If this has been true in the past, it is likely to be true of all your present and future worries. So if you find that you are worrying about a thing today, the chances are nine to one that it will not eventuate as your fears anticipate. We all must gamble a little and take our chances with the future. The worrier is a stupid gambler who takes his gains playing his hand for losses.

Fifth, you can learn to give up worrying. But do not expect a sudden transformation of mental habits. Since worrying is acquired by practice, you will have to undo the habit by practice in the opposite direction. Begin where the going might be easiest and most likely to issue successfully, viz., with minor incidents and situations. When you have learned to cope calmly with minor difficulties, you can move forward and gradually extend your improved mental attitude to other problems which confront you. If you find the the initial effort very difficult, you may try to confine your worrying to some particular part of the day, leaving the rest free for things that are constructive and sensible. If you must get your worrying in, one hour in the morning ought to be sufficient. Any kind of progress toward the ultimate goal is encouraging. Anyone who is devoting less time to worrying, or is worrying about fewer things than formerly, is really making progress.

A DAY AT A TIME

Live one day at a time. This does not mean that the problems and necessities of tomorrow should not be anticipated today. But it does mean that when the future has been provided for as well and sensibly as is humanly possible, your attention and energy should bear down squarely upon the problems and duties of today, without anxiety for tomorrow or regret for yesterday. If your mind is burdened with reliving the errors of the past and anticipating the responsibilities of the future while you are employed with the cares of the present, you are overloaded with a triple burden. This is really the work of three persons.

Proceed in this matter in a positive, resolute fashion. Set about the work you have to do today and do it vigorously to the best of your present ability. Make the fulfillment of today's task a glorious, absorbing obsession. When it is done, the morrow will be waiting with its work. But do not cross the bridge till you reach it.

DECISION

Learn to make decisions quickly and firmly. Occasions arrive every day when you are forced to make a choice between rival alternatives of action. Sometimes the matter is important, like a decision concerning one's vocation or accepting a proposal of marriage. Sometimes it is unimportant, e.g., whether to go to the bank this morning or this afternoon, whether to go to a show or to stay at home, whether to wear a blue necktie or a red one, etc. In all such cases we arrive at a mental crossroad, and a decision must be made one way or the other, even if the matter is unimportant. We can't debate the matter forever.

When the rival alternatives of action are more or less evenly balanced, the necessity of arriving at a practical decision sometimes brings on an uneasy, annoying suspense. In certain cases, the inability to make a satisfactory decision in the presence of a need to make one creates a sense of distress and panicky helplessness. And each new endeavor to break the deadlock seems merely to prolong and aggravate the mental exasperation. Everyone has experienced, to some extent, this mental fretfulness which follows in the path of hesitancy and indecision.

Caught in such a dilemma one may simply defer the decision for no other reason than to avoid the bother of making up his mind immediately. This is merely an unstrategic retreat. It does not settle the issue but merely saves up another bother for tomorrow. If the matter is of no grave importance, there is absolutely no need of a prolonged deliberation or any postponement of decision. Simply size up the situation callously and coolly and make up your mind on the spot with disrespectful abandon. Since the match is even, seize one or the other of the alternatives with utter recklessness and think of the issue as definitely closed. If you want to make the matter interesting, break the deadlock by tossing a coin or cutting cards. This is an especially agreeable means of unbolting a deadlock if it involves two or more persons interested in but unable to reach a common decision. For in many cases when one frets about making a choice, it really does not make any difference which one is made. Besides, this sensitive hesitancy about deciding matters of minor importance is sometimes due to an overwrought fastidiousness or to an exaggerated eagerness to be right—both marks of vanity and neither are respectable character traits to be encouraged.

However, if the matter for decision is actually one of importance, consider the pros and cons, taking the care and leisure which it deserves. Then if the proper decision is not obvious, pigeonhole the entire affair and leave it rest for a while. *Definitely decide immediately not to settle the issue then.* Treat it as unfinished business to be reconsidered at a future time. During the interim do not agitate yourself about it. Think about it as little as possible. Such a deferment of decision is not a weak retreat. It is a strategic delay decreed with the expectation of reinforcements. During the interim of delay, new evidence, additional light or some fresh inspiration may arrive which will enable you to make the decision without effort. Many hard perplexities melt away if you only give them time. But if it comes to the point where the decision must be made without further delay and the bidding alternatives are still matched in even competition, bravely stake your chances on one or the other at random and consider the matter closed for good. What else is there to do? It may be the wrong decision, but as far as you know it has just as many chances to be right as wrong. No one can entirely deliver life from the perils of chance.

Then there is such a thing as making a decision quickly enough but not firmly enough. This happens when the decision is made but feebly clung to with a kind of regretful suspicion that the other alternative might, after all, have been the better one. Although the choice is made, it always seems to be in peril of being revoked.

Some people seem to make nearly all their decisions, even in affairs of trivial importance, with this kind of timid semifinality. They never seem to arrive with decisions clean of remorse. As a consequence they live in a mental atmosphere of uneasiness and self-reproach. A firm decision burns the bridges behind it. Once a choice has been made, think of it as the only choice that could have been made and treat all its former competitors as never having existed. Occasionally, however, a decision ought to be reconsidered and, perhaps, revoked. But never entertain the prospect of a reconsideration unless there is some clear and definite indication that you have made a mistake. It is only stubbornness or pride that clings to a choice merely because it has been made. If it is clear upon reconsideration that the previous decision should be revoked or corrected, make the change at once, but firmly and without regret. From time to time, every sensible person must avow his mistakes and rearrange his judgments in the interests of honesty.

There are times when one clearly foresees that a certain decision will entail unpleasant reactions for himself or painful consequences for others. In such cases one may clearly understand what decision *ought* to be made and yet hesitate or refuse to make it because of future consequences. Such hesitancy or refusal to decide is not so much an inability to make up one's mind as it is a fear of declaring it. This sort of indecision is a moral, not a mental, difficulty. To waver in making a decision which we know is right and which is our duty to make is obviously a defect of character which ought to be called moral cowardice.

HUMOR

Promote a sense of humor. This does not mean assembling a repertoire of jokes and funny stories to dispense on appropriate occasions. Many parlor entertainers are quite deficient in genuine humor. They may be merely hollow trumpets of somebody else's humor. Genuine humor is the ability to recognize and enjoy the funny incongruities and inconsistencies that lurk in the situations and predicaments of everyday life, even if these incongruities and inconsistencies appear in oneself.

A person with humor really enjoys life in a way that is unknown to one without it. It releases one from the tension of overwrought seriousness, balances judgment and corrects perspective, softens the asperities of life and cushions one against the jolts of daily existence. It is a lubricant which eases the friction of daily strife and combat. It puts others at ease and invites their sympathy and cooperation. But its principal blessing may be that it helps to save one from the tragic blunder of taking himself too seriously. I think it is Father Faber who says that humor may be a "special grace of God." At any rate it offers a kindly service in the spiritual realm by smoothing down scruples and softening the blows of daily temptations to evil. For even certain temptations to moral wrongdoing, when viewed in retrospect, are outright ludicrous. Even the devil has his funny angles and is best handled if treated with good-natured mirth. All in all, a genial spirit of humor creates an atmosphere which is very favorable for the growth of many virtues.

Perhaps humor is an innate quality or perhaps it is an acquired trait. But very few people, I believe, are entirely bereft of it. Perhaps it may be smothered and crushed out. But certainly it can be fostered and encouraged. At any rate, preserve the spirit of gracious humor, for it ranks important as a preservative of mental health and spiritual vigor.

CANDOR

Cultivate the habit of absolute intellectual candor. In other words, face the facts, especially when your own interest and prestige are concerned and admit them at once. If you are a homely, inefficient, lazy wretch, do not attempt to think of yourself as a model of beauty, effi-

ciency and energy. Recognize your own deficiency without attempting
to blur the vision. You need not, of course, display your defects to
others, but you should admit them to yourself. Admit them also to
others if they call your attention to them. "It is better to be rebuked by
a wise man than to be deceived by the flattery of fools." (Eccles. 7:6)

Failure to recognize yourself squarely as you are leads gradually to
many kinds of unhealthy quirks of character, which the psychologist
calls "defense mechanisms," like inventing subterfuges, blaming others
for your own failures, daydreaming, rationalizing your conduct, delusions
of greatness and lying. All of these mechanisms are underhand tricks
which an unhealthy mind invents to evade the truth about itself. You
can avoid all of these deviations from mental wholesomeness by acquiring the habit of recognizing and admitting your own deficiencies and
faults without whimpering or trying to establish an alibi. It is wonderful
how free and joyous one feels when he once gives up the bunkum of
making himself out to be right when he knows that he is wrong.

You should not, of course, be content with your deficiencies and
faults. Recognizing and admitting their existence is a necessary condition
for their correction. You cannot correct or eradicate a defect by hiding
or defending it, or by pretending to yourself that it does not exist. You
cannot move one step toward self-improvement, mental or moral, unless
you open your eyes widely and candidly to your own deficiencies. This
is one of the first principles of practical psychiatry and spiritual direction.

Suggestions

1. Draw up four health rules which you intend to keep for life.
2. Discuss how the character of games and the manner of recreation
   should vary with age.
3. Have you a hobby? What sort of hobby is especially suitable for a
   student or for one engaged in the profession or business which you
   expect to pursue?
4. From your own experience give a practical example of useless indecision.
5. In what particular way do you exhibit a lack of candor? What is
   intellectual candor? Explain how it manifests itself.
6. What suggestion about mental health contained in this chapter do
   you regard most helpful for yourself?
7. Read Lockington's *Bodily Health and Spiritual Vigor*.
8. Read a simple, sensible book on mental health. Consult McCarthy's
   Safeguarding Mental Health, McLaughlin's *Personal Hygiene*, Pratt's
   Your Mind and You and Williams's *Mental Hygiene and the College
   Student* (pamphlet).

Reading List

The following is a list of books which the author regards as useful to assist the student in his profession of studying. Each book in the list treats some phase of the work of a student. Some of them are extensive treatments of matters which have been only briefly touched in the present volume. The inclusion of a book in this list is not to be interpreted as expressing the author's satisfaction or agreement with everything the book contains.

Adler, Mortimer J. *How to Read a Book.* Simon & Schuster, Inc., N.Y.

Bennett, M. E. *College and Life.* McGraw-Hill Book Co., N.Y.

Bird, Charles. *Effective Study Habits.* D. Appleton-Century Co., N.Y.

Broening, Angela et al. *Reading for Skill.*

Book, William F. *Learning How to Study and Work Effectively.* Ginn and Co., Mass.

*Chappell, Matthew N. *In the Name of Common Sense.* Macmillan Publishing Co., Inc., N.Y.

Clippinger, Walter D. *Student Relationships.* Thom. Nelson and Sons, N.Y.

Cole, Luella. *Improvement of Reading.* Farrar, Straus & Giroux, Inc., N.Y.

Crawley, S. L. *Studying Efficiently.* Prentice-Hall Inc., N.J.

Dimnet, Ernest. *The Art of Thinking.* Simon & Schuster, Inc., N.Y.

Garesche, Edward F. *Training for Life.* P. J. Kenedy and Sons, N.Y.

Gavit, John Palmer. *College.* Harcourt Brace Jovanovich, Inc., N.Y.

Greenough, James Bradstreet. *Words and Their Ways in English Speech.* Macmillan Publishing Co., N.Y.

Groves, Ernest R. *Personality and Social Adjustment.* Longmans, Green and Co., N.Y.

Harris, A. J. *How to Increase Reading Ability.* Longmans, Green and Co., N.Y.

Headley, Leal A. *How to Study in College.* Henry Holt and Co., N.Y.

James, William. *Talks to Teachers on Psychology and to Students on Some of Life's Ideals.* Henry Holt and Co., N.Y.

*An excellent book for worriers.

Jones, Edward S. *Improvement of Study Habits.* Henry Stewart Inc., N.Y.

Lockington, William J. *Bodily Health and Spiritual Vigour.* Longmans, Green and Co., N.Y.

Lyman, Rollo LaVerne. *Method of Study.* Scott, Foresman & Co., Ill.

McCarthy, R. C. *Safeguarding Mental Health.* Bruce Publishing Co., Milwaukee, Wis.

McLaughlin, A. J. *Personal Hygiene.* Funk and Wagnalls Co., N.Y.

McMurry, F. M. *How to Study and Teaching How to Study.* Houghton Mifflin Co., Boston, N.Y., and Chicago.

Matthews, Brander. *Essays on English.* Houghton Mifflin Co., Boston, N.Y., and Chicago.

Miltner, Charles. *Progressive Ignorance.* Herder Book Co., Mo. (Cf. chapters "A Live Mind," p. 31, "The Art of Forgettng," p. 39.)

O'Brien, John A. *Reading.* Century Publishing Co., N.Y.

Pratt, G. K. *Your Mind and You.* Funk and Wagnalls Co., N.Y.

Quiller-Couch, A. T. *On the Art of Reading.* G. P. Putnam's Sons, N.Y.

Robbins, Charles L. *Will to Work.*

Sandrick, Richard Lanning. *How to Study and What to Study.* D. C. Heath and Co., Mass.

Seidel, Henry. *On Reading Fiercely.* Chapter from Kaufmann's *Points of View for College Students,* Doubleday, Page and Co., N.Y.

Smith, S. Stephenson. *The Command of Words.* Thomas Y. Crowell Co., N.Y.

Starke, D. *Mental Efficiency Series.* (Ten small volumes.) Funk and Wagnalls Co., N.Y.

Stone, Clarence R. *Silent and Oral Reading.* Houghton Mifflin Co., Boston, N.Y., and Chicago.

Trench, Richard Chenevix. *On the Study of Words.* Macmillan Publishing Co., N.Y.

Whipple, Guy Montrose. *How to Study Effectively.* Public School Pub. Co., Ill.

White, Richard Grant. *Words and Their Uses.* Sheldon and Co., N.Y.

Wiliam, F. E. *Mental Hygiene and the College Student.* (Pamphlet.) National Committee for Mental Hygiene, N.Y.

Wrenn, C. Gilbert and Cole, Luella. *Reading Rapidly and Well.* Stanford University Press, California.